This revision guide is matched to the new single award **AQA GCSE Additional Applied Science specification (4863)**.

The assessment for this specification comprises three units: two portfolio units, and one unit which is assessed externally by a written exam. An overview of the three units is provided at the foot of this page.

This revision guide provides full coverage of the exam-assessed unit (Unit 2) and some information about working safely in science. Although this revision guide does not directly cover Unit 1 or Unit 3, the information provided should help you to complete the reports for your portfolios.

Unit 2 is divided into three specific areas in which scientists can work. In this guide, they are colour-coded for easy reference: Food Science is green, Forensic Science is orange, and Sports Science is blue.

For each section, the AQA GCSE Additional Applied Science specification identifies some techniques that are used by food scientists, forensic scientists and sports scientists. You need to demonstrate an understanding of these techniques in your reports and in the exam.

This guide can be used to revise for both the Foundation and the Higher Tier exams. No differentiation is made in the content. However, the questions in the Higher Tier exam will be more demanding.

Some spellings within this guide differ from the British standard to correspond to those that are on the specification and that will appear in your exam.

This guide is intended revision material for GCSE students, but it is our hope that it will also ease the burden of over-worked science departments.

How to Use this Revision Guide

This guide contains everything you need to know in a user-friendly format. In certain places we have included slightly more than the specification suggests you need to know in order to aid your understanding.

Do not just read the guide – learn actively! Constantly test yourself without looking at the text.

Jot down anything you think will help you to revise, no matter how trivial it may seem.

About the Author

Silvia Newton worked as a science teacher and examiner for 25 years before becoming a freelance science consultant. She has been heavily involved with a variety of science website projects, as well as contributing to a number of science publications.

Project Editor: Rachael Hemsley
Cover and Concept Design: Sarah Duxbury
Designer: Richard Arundale
Artwork: Lonsdale and HL Studios

ISBN-10: 1-905129-67-X
ISBN-13: 978-1-905129-67-6

Published by Lonsdale, a division of Huveaux Plc

Unit	What is Being Assessed?	How is it Assessed?	Weighting	Total Marks
Unit 1	Science in the Workplace	Portfolio (2 reports)	20%	25 marks
Unit 2	Science at Work	1-hour written exam	40%	60 marks
Unit 3	Using Scientific Skills	Portfolio (1 report)	40%	40 marks

Contents

Contents

The reference numbers in brackets correspond to the reference numbers on the AQA GCSE Additional Applied Science specification.

Portfolios Overview

Science in the Workplace (Unit 1)

Scientific theories and techniques are used by many people in a wide variety of jobs. For this unit, you will need to use your research skills to investigate science in the workplace and produce a portfolio of evidence which will be marked by your teacher(s).

Your portfolio needs to include two reports:

Investigating How Science is Used

You will need to investigate workplaces that use scientific skills. Your report should include descriptions of…

- the products made, or services provided, by the organisations, and their importance to society
- how science is used in a wide variety of jobs and workplaces
- the type of work the scientists (or people who use scientific skills) carry out in the workplace
- the skills and qualifications that the scientists need to possess
- the effect that the organisations have on the local environment.

Working Safely in Science

You will need to undertake an investigation into working safely in a scientific workplace. Your report should include descriptions of…

- the health and safety checks that are carried out in the workplace
- hazards and risks and how they can be assessed
- first aid procedures
- fire prevention procedures and how to deal with fires
- how safety precautions in the workplace compare with those in your school or college.

Written communication is specifically assessed in this unit, so your portfolio needs to show that you can…

- use a variety of sources of information
- present your findings in a clear and logical way.

Remember, this portfolio is worth 25 marks, and accounts for 20% of your total mark.

Using Scientific Skills (Unit 3)

For this unit you need to produce a portfolio of evidence which will be marked by your teacher(s).

Your portfolio of evidence should contain a report of a practical investigation from **one** of the three applied science areas you have studied: Food Science, Forensic Science and Sports Science.

Your report should show that you are able to…

- explain the purpose (vocational relevance) of your investigation
- produce a plan of your investigation
- produce a risk assessment
- choose appropriate equipment
- carry out your plan safely
- collect and record relevant information accurately, and repeat measurements if necessary
- present the information appropriately
- use scientific knowledge to interpret your results and draw conclusions from your investigation
- evaluate your investigation (i.e. describe its strengths and weaknesses) and suggest improvements to allow you to collect more accurate and reliable evidence
- explain how your findings could be used and applied by a food scientist, a forensic scientist or a sports scientist.

In the specification you will find a list of investigations for each area of applied science, to give you some ideas for your investigation.

Remember, this unit is worth 40 marks and accounts for 40% of your total marks.

Working Safely in Science

Hazards and Risks

All workplaces have health and safety regulations to ensure that workers are not exposed to undue risks, and to minimise the chance of accidents happening.

Scientific work can be dangerous, yet accidents are rare because scientists are aware of the **hazards** they deal with, and of the need to work safely.

A hazard is something (e.g. a substance, equipment or an activity) that could cause harm. Hazards in scientific workplaces include…

- not using protective and safety equipment
- not using equipment properly
- not following correct procedures
- using substances classified as toxic, flammable, corrosive, oxidising, harmful, irritant or radioactive
- using microorganisms
- using utilities, e.g. gas and electricity.

Hazards are identified by **symbols** that have specific meanings (see opposite).

A **risk** is the likelihood that a hazard will cause harm. If the hazards and their possible dangers can be recognised, the risk can be reduced or eliminated.

A **risk assessment** identifies all the hazards and risks that may cause harm during an activity, together with the **control measures** that may be taken to reduce the risk.

Hazard	Symbol
Biohazard Risk of contamination or infection. *Examples: E. coli (bacteria), HIV (virus).*	
Corrosive Burns and destroys materials and living tissues, including eyes and skin, on contact. *Example: sulfuric acid.*	
Flammable Catches fire easily. *Example: petrol.*	
Harmful Similar to toxic; enters the body in the same way, but much larger doses are needed to cause harm. *Examples: petrol, methylated spirits.*	
Irritant Can cause reddening or blistering of the skin. *Example: bleach.*	
Oxidising Provides oxygen, which allows other materials to burn more easily. *Example: liquid oxygen.*	
Radiation Risk of radioactive emission. *Examples: X-rays, gamma rays.*	
Toxic Can cause death if inhaled, swallowed or taken in through the skin. *Example: cyanide.*	

Working Safely in Science

First Aid

It is important that you know how to carry out basic **first aid** in case an accident happens in the laboratory or workplace.

You can receive training for **first aid qualifications** from St. John Ambulance and British Red Cross.

Below are some examples of accidents that you may come across in the laboratory or workplace, together with instructions on how to deal with them.

Heat Burns and Scalds

Burns are caused by dry heat. Scalds are caused by wet heat.

To treat a burn or a scald, you should:
1. Cool the affected area gently for about 10 minutes using cold water.
2. Loosely cover the burn or scald with a clean, non-fluffy dressing or sheet, and secure using medical tape. Do not use adhesive dressings.

Chemical Burns

Chemical burns are caused by acids, alkalis or other chemicals. The 'burn' is the result of the chemical destroying body tissues. The skin may appear red and there may be a stinging feeling.

To treat a chemical burn, you should:
1. Wash the area with large amounts of cold water for 10 minutes, e.g. under a running tap or shower.
2. Seek medical assistance.

Breathing in Fumes

Fumes are the gases given off from chemicals and fires.

If you breath in fumes, you should:
1. Leave the area and go into fresh air.
2. Seek medical assistance immediately.

Swallowing Chemicals

If you get chemicals in your mouth, you should:
1. Spit them out immediately and wash out your mouth with water.
2. Identify the chemical that has been swallowed.
3. Seek medical assistance immediately.

Electric Shock

An electric shock is caused when an electric current passes through the body. It may happen if a person has wet hands or is standing on a wet floor while using electrical equipment. Symptoms of electric shock include pale, cold skin, sweating, feeling sick and loss of consciousness.

If you are treating someone who has suffered an electric shock, you should:
1. Take care for your own safety, and make sure the casualty is no longer in contact with the source of electricity. Switch off the mains supply before removing the plug from the socket.
2. If the casualty is unconscious but still breathing, place him / her in the recovery position.
3. If the casualty is unconscious and not breathing, prepare to resuscitate him / her.
4. Seek medical assistance immediately.

Eye Accidents

You need to be very careful when treating damaged eyes.

If you have got **chemicals** in your eye, you should:
1. Wash the eye with a large quantity of gently running water for at least 10 minutes.
2. Seek medical assistance.

If you have got **particles** in your eye, you should:
1. Wash the eye with gently running water.
2. If this does not remove the particles, seek medical assistance.

If the particle (e.g. a fragment of glass) is embedded in the eye, you should:
1. Loosely cover both eyes with sterile eye pads to reduce eye movement.
2. Seek medical assistance.

Fire Prevention

Fires need **oxygen**, **fuel** and **heat** in order to burn. Removing one of these components can prevent fires spreading.

The Fire Triangle

Oxygen

Fuel   Heat

Fire Procedures

If you hear a fire alarm or smoke alarm, you should:

1. Respond immediately.
2. Make sure any heat sources, such as Bunsen burners, are turned off.
3. Close all doors and windows.
4. Evacuate the building by the nearest exit.
5. Assemble in the area that has been assigned to you.

If you find a fire, you should:

1. Raise the alarm immediately.
2. Make sure any heat sources, such as Bunsen burners, are turned off.
3. Assess the situation from a safe distance.
4. If the fire is small, make one attempt to tackle it with the appropriate fire extinguisher (see opposite) or fire blanket.
5. Leave the room as quickly as possible, making sure that all other people have left.

Types of Fires

When tackling a fire, the first thing to do is to prevent more fuel reaching the fire, in order to stop it spreading. A **fire extinguisher** cools the fire down or stops oxygen getting to it.

Fires are divided into four **classes** according to the type of material that is burning. The class of fire determines how it should be treated and whether it should only be dealt with by a professional firefighter (see table).

Fire Class	Type of Material	Action to be Taken
A	Solid carbon compounds	Use a water or foam extinguisher.
B	Flammable liquids	Use a foam, carbon dioxide or dry powder extinguisher.
C	Flammable gases	Turn off fuel or gas supply. Do not attempt to tackle. Call fire brigade.
D	Flammable metals	Do not attempt to tackle. Call fire brigade.
Electrical	Electrical equipment	Use a carbon dioxide or dry powder extinguisher.

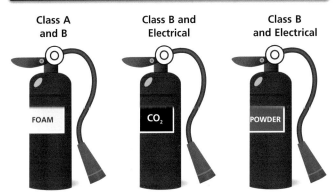

Class A and B — FOAM

Class B and Electrical — CO₂

Class B and Electrical — POWDER

Fire blankets can be used on electrical fires, or on someone whose clothes are on fire. They are made from non-flammable materials, and work by cutting off the oxygen supply.

Most public buildings have the following safety features to prevent fires spreading:

- **Automatic sprinkler systems** turn on when the temperature reaches a pre-set level (usually 65°C). Individual sprinkler heads on the ceiling open when a solder link melts or a liquid-filled glass bulb breaks, and a spray of water is then released over the source of heat.
- **Fire doors** prevent the spread of fire and smoke. They may be made of steel or solid wood. Many close automatically. You should never wedge or prop open fire doors.

Food Science

Food Nutrients and Their Functions

The human body needs different nutrients in order to carry out the vital functions of life. You need to know about the…

- sources and functions of the nutrients, including vitamins, minerals and fibre
- symptoms of some vitamin deficiencies
- importance of a balanced diet
- health risks associated with some foods.

The Food Standards Agency

The **Food Standards Agency (FSA)** is the independent food safety watchdog set up by an Act of Parliament in 2000. It protects the public's health and consumer interests in relation to food. The FSA employs **food scientists** and **dieticians** who work to promote good eating habits, and ensure that food is labelled correctly and safe to eat.

Food scientists analyse food in order to find out…
- which nutrients are present (**qualitative analysis**, see p.19)
- how much of each nutrient is present (**quantitative analysis**, see p.20).

Dieticians investigate a person's food intake (diet) to find out how much of each nutrient is being consumed, and recommend how the diet can be made healthier.

Nutrients

We need food for movement, growth and repair of tissues, respiration and good health.

A healthy diet contains seven different **nutrients**:
- carbohydrates (see opposite)
- proteins (see p.9)
- fats (see p.10)
- vitamins (see p.11–12)
- minerals (see p.13)
- water (see p.14)
- fibre (see p.14).

Carbohydrates

Carbohydrates are fuels that provide the body with **energy**. They are compounds of carbon, hydrogen and oxygen. There are two types of carbohydrates: **simple** and **complex**.

Simple Carbohydrates
Simple carbohydrates include **sugars**, of which there are different types:
- **Fructose** can be found in many fruits.
- **Lactose** is the sugar found in milk.
- **Sucrose** is the sugar that is put in tea.
- **Glucose** is the sugar that the body uses in respiration.

Sugars like glucose and fructose are examples of **monosaccharides** (monomers).

A **disaccharide** is a sugar composed of two monosaccharides; for example, sucrose is formed when fructose and glucose are joined together.

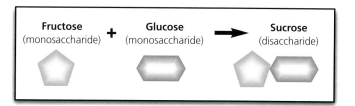

Complex Carbohydrates
Complex carbohydrates, or **polysaccharides**, are made of many monosaccharides joined together. For example, **starch** is a complex carbohydrate because it is a large molecule made of lots of glucose molecules joined together. Starch is found in foods like bread, cereal, rice, pasta, potatoes, oats and beans.

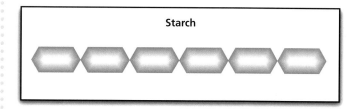

Glycogen is another complex carbohydrate. It is a large molecule made up of lots of glucose molecules joined together. It is stored in the liver and muscles. Our bodies change glycogen to glucose in order to provide energy when we need it.

Iodine Test for Starch

To test if starch is present in a food sample, add a few drops of iodine solution to the sample (which can be solid or liquid). If starch is present, the brownish yellow iodine solution changes colour to blue–black.

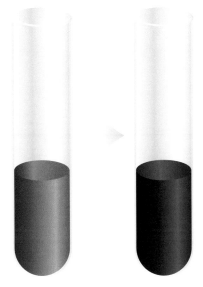

Benedict's Test for Glucose

Glucose is known as a reducing sugar because it reduces blue copper sulfate to orange copper oxide. To test if glucose is present in a food sample:

1 Mash up the sample, if it is not a liquid.
2 Put a little of the sample into a test tube and add water until the tube is one-third full.
3 Add Benedict's solution.
4 Heat the test tube to 80°C.

If glucose is present, a yellow, green or orange precipitate appears.

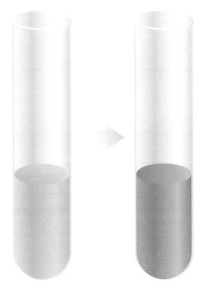

Proteins

The human body is made up of cells, which are mainly **protein**. During **growth** the body needs protein in order to make new cells. Protein is also needed by the body to repair old or damaged cells.

Proteins are compounds of carbon, hydrogen, oxygen and nitrogen. They are large molecules made up of lots of **amino acid** molecules joined together.

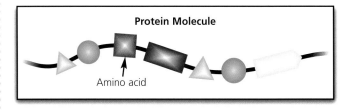

Protein Molecule

Amino acid

Some foods that are rich in protein are meat, fish, dairy foods, (e.g. milk, cheese), eggs, beans, lentils and nuts.

Biuret Test for Protein

To test if protein is present in a food sample:

1 Mash up the sample, if it is not a liquid.
2 Put a spatula of the sample into a test tube and add water until the tube is one-third full.
3 Add a few drops of sodium hydroxide (NaOH) solution and shake the test tube gently.
4 Add a few drops of copper sulfate ($CuSO_4$) solution.

If protein is present, the copper sulfate changes colour from blue to purple.

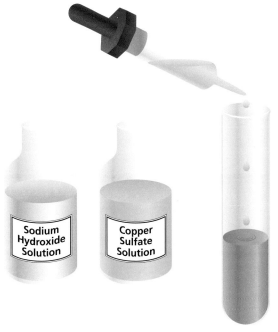

Sodium Hydroxide Solution

Copper Sulfate Solution

Food Science

Fats

Fats provide the body with energy – they contain more energy than carbohydrates.

Our bodies store fats under the skin to use when we are short of energy. Fats are good **insulators**, so they reduce heat loss from the body. A layer of fat surrounds and protects many of the body's vital organs, such as the kidneys.

Fats also provide fat-soluble vitamins, e.g. vitamins A, D and K.

Fats are compounds of carbon, hydrogen and oxygen. At room temperature, fats are solid and oils are liquid. A fat or oil is made of three molecules of fatty acids joined to a molecule of glycerol (see diagram opposite).

Different fats have different kinds of fatty acids (see diagram opposite):

- If the fatty acids contain no **double bonds** they are **saturated** fatty acids.
- If the fatty acids contain one double bond they are **monounsaturated** fatty acids.
- If the fatty acids contain two or more double bonds they are **polyunsaturated** fatty acids.

Saturated fats are found in meat, oily fish (for example, tuna, salmon and mackerel), eggs, butter, cheese and cream.

Unsaturated fats are found in olives, olive oil, sunflower oil, seeds and nuts (for example, peanuts and walnuts).

Alcohol Emulsion Test for Fat

To test if fat is present in a food sample:

1 Put a small piece of the sample into a test tube. Add a little ethanol (ethyl alcohol) and shake the test tube.

2 Add a little water (roughly the same amount as ethanol) to the test tube.

If fat is present, a milky white emulsion forms (see diagram opposite).

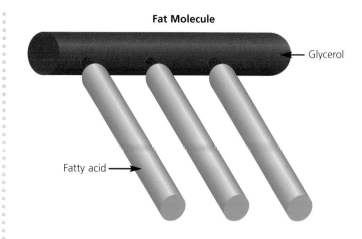

Fat Molecule

Glycerol

Fatty acid

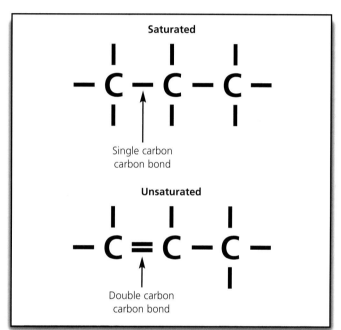

Saturated

Single carbon carbon bond

Unsaturated

Double carbon carbon bond

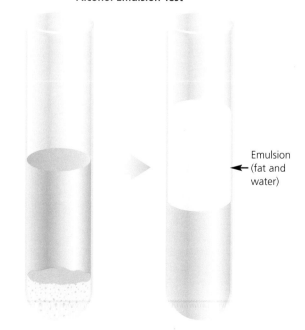

Alcohol Emulsion Test

Emulsion (fat and water)

Vitamins

Vitamins are essential for good health. Your body needs small, regular amounts of vitamins, which you need to get through your diet. If you do not get the vitamins your body needs, you can become very ill.

Vitamins are either fat soluble or water soluble.

The table below lists the vitamins you need to know about:

Vitamin	Sources	Function(s)	Symptom(s) of Deficiency
Vitamin A – fat soluble	• Cheese • Eggs • Liver • Margarine • Milk • Oily fish, e.g. mackerel • Yoghurt	• Good eyesight • Keeps a healthy mucous membrane lining in organs (e.g. the nose)	• Poor night vision (i.e. the eyes are unable to adjust to dim light) • Dry skin and mucous membranes
Vitamin B Group – water soluble	• Cereals • Eggs • Liver • Yeast	• Aids the release of energy from carbohydrates in respiration • Haemoglobin for red blood cells • Keeps nervous system healthy	• Mouth sores • Anaemia • Nerve-cell degeneration
Vitamin C (ascorbic acid) – water soluble	• Fruit • Vegetables	• Maintains a healthy immune system • Keeps skin and the linings of the digestive system (epithelium) healthy • Aids the absorption of iron from food	• Scurvy (bleeding gums, cracked skin, cuts and wounds that do not heal) • Weakening of blood vessels
Vitamin D – fat soluble	• Cheese • Eggs • Liver • Milk • Oily fish • Made by your skin in sunlight	• Keeps teeth and bones strong • Aids the absorption of calcium and phosphorus from food	• Soft teeth • Soft bones, which may bend due to excess body weight (rickets)
Vitamin K – fat soluble	• Green leafy vegetables, e.g. broccoli, spinach	• Helps blood to clot	• Poor clotting of blood

Food Science

Vitamins (cont.)

Finding the Amount of Vitamin C in Fruit Juice

To find the amount of vitamin C in a food sample, e.g. fruit juice:

1 Dissolve a known amount of vitamin C in water to make a **standard solution**.

2 Prepare a set of standard solutions, each containing different concentrations of vitamin C.

3 Measure out 20cm³ of the first standard solution of vitamin C into a flask.

4 Carry out a **titration** to find the volume of DCPIP that is decolourised by the first standard solution of vitamin C.

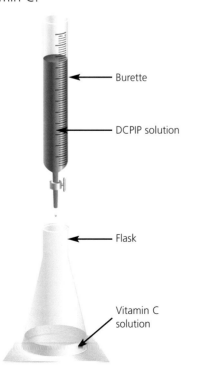

Burette

DCPIP solution

Flask

Vitamin C solution

5 Repeat the titration for the rest of the standard solutions of vitamin C using the same volume (20cm³) of vitamin C solution each time.

6 Use the information to draw a graph.

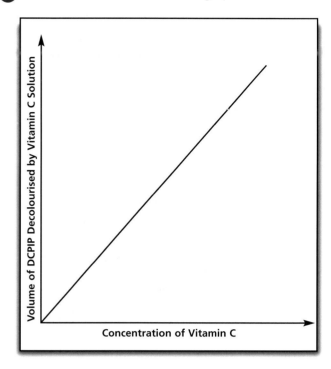

Volume of DCPIP Decolourised by Vitamin C Solution

Concentration of Vitamin C

7 Using 20cm³ of a sample of fruit juice, carry out a titration to find the volume of DCPIP that is decolourised by it. Then use the graph to find out the concentration of vitamin C in the sample (see red line on graph).

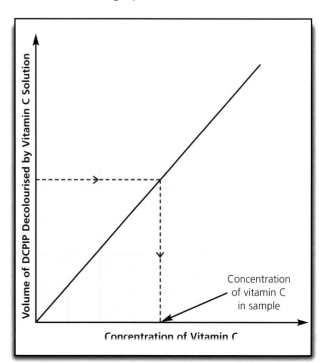

Volume of DCPIP Decolourised by Vitamin C Solution

Concentration of vitamin C in sample

Concentration of Vitamin C

Minerals

Your body needs small, regular amounts of **minerals**. If they are missing from your diet you can become ill.

Mineral	Sources	Function
Iron	Cocoa, liver, red meat, spinach	To make haemoglobin for red blood cells
Calcium	Cheese, green vegetables, milk	For healthy bones, teeth and nails
Phosphorus	Most foods including dairy, eggs, meat, vegetables	Helps to release energy from food in respiration
Zinc	Fish, liver, shellfish	For enzyme action and healing wounds

Finding the Amount of Iron in a Food Sample

To find out how much iron is in a food sample:

1. Dissolve a known amount of iron chloride ($FeCl_3$) in water to make a standard solution.
2. Prepare a set of standard solutions, each containing different concentrations of iron chloride.
3. Add 5cm³ potassium thiocyanate solution to 100cm³ of each standard solution. The colourless thiocyanate ions react with any Fe^{3+} ions present. The intensity of the red colour is proportional to the number of Fe^{3+} ions in the solution.

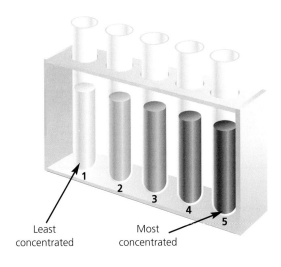

Least concentrated   Most concentrated

4. Find the mass of the food sample and place it in a crucible.
5. Heat the crucible strongly until only grey–white mineral ash is left.
6. After the ash has cooled, transfer it to a test tube and add 5cm³ hydrochloric acid ($HCl_{(aq)}$).
7. Add 95cm³ water and 5cm³ potassium thiocyanate solution to the test tube.
8. Compare the red colour of the sample to the colour of the standard solutions to find the percentage of iron present in the food sample.

For example, if the colour in the sample test tube matches the colour in standard solution test tube 3, the concentration of iron (Fe^{3+}) is the same.

A more accurate method is to use a **colorimeter** to measure the amount of light passing through each standard solution. This information can then be used to plot a graph.

Then, using the colorimeter, measure the amount of light passing through the sample solution. The concentration of Fe^{3+} ions present can be found by using the graph.

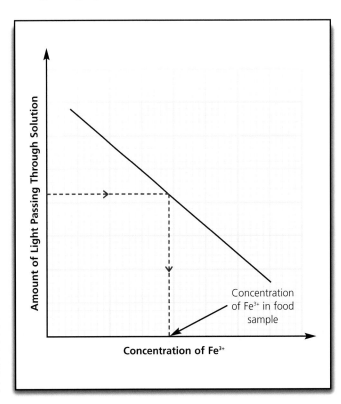

Food Science

Water

Water makes up about 70% of a person's body weight. Water is taken in by eating and drinking.

Water is needed…
- in cells as chemical reactions take place in water
- to transport waste chemicals, e.g. urea, out of the body
- to transport dissolved substances, e.g. glucose, around the body
- to cool the body, when it evaporates as sweat.

Finding the Amount of Water in a Food Sample

To find the amount of water in a food sample:

1 Find the mass of an empty crucible.

2 Put the food sample in the crucible and find the total mass.

3 Calculate the mass of the food sample.

4 Leave the crucible in an oven set at 90°C for a few days.

5 Find the new mass of the crucible and food.

6 Repeat steps 4 and 5 until a constant mass is obtained.

7 Work out the percentage of water in the food sample using the following formula:

$$\text{Percentage mass of water in food} = \frac{\text{Initial mass} - \text{Final mass}}{\text{Initial mass}} \times 100$$

Example

Find the percentage mass of water in an apple sample if the initial mass is 16.5g and the dried mass is 4.7g.

Use the equation…

$$\text{Percentage mass of water in apple} = \frac{16.5 - 4.7}{16.5} \times 100$$

$$= \frac{11.8}{16.5} \times 100$$

$$= \textbf{71.5\%}$$

Fibre

Fibre adds bulk to food. Dietary fibre (**roughage**) comes from the **cellulose** in plant cell walls. The body cannot digest cellulose because it does not make the required enzymes, so the fibre passes through the gut. This gives the muscles of the gut something to push against as food is moved through the intestine. If not enough fibre is present in a person's diet, the contents of the gut do not keep moving, and this results in **constipation**.

Fibre can be found in wholemeal bread, beans, fruit and vegetables, and in some breakfast cereals.

To find the amount of fibre in a food, see p.21.

Diet and Health

A **balanced diet** contains the right amount of the seven nutrients (see diagram below).

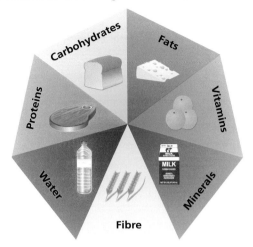

The amount of **energy** a person needs each day depends on…
- his / her body size
- how active he / she is
- how fast he / she is growing.

It is important that a person gets the right amount of energy each day (see graph below). Energy is measured in **kilojoules** (**kJ**, 1kJ = 1000J).

If a person's energy intake is lower than required, he / she will become too thin; this could be a sign of **anorexia nervosa**.

If a person's energy intake is higher than required, he / she will become overweight or **obese**, particularly if he / she does not exercise enough. If a person is obese, he / she will have an increased risk of getting **heart disease** and / or **diabetes**.

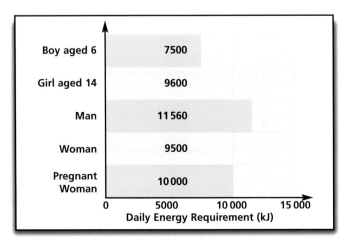

	Daily Energy Requirement (kJ)
Boy aged 6	7500
Girl aged 14	9600
Man	11 560
Woman	9500
Pregnant Woman	10 000

A person is **malnourished** if his / her diet is not balanced, for example…
- a diet that contains too much **salt** can cause **high blood pressure** which is a major cause of **heart disease** and **strokes**
- a diet that contains too much **sugar** can cause obesity and an increased risk of heart disease and diabetes
- a diet that contains too much **saturated fat** makes the level of **cholesterol** in the blood go up.

Cholesterol sticks to the inside of blood vessels making them narrower. This reduces the flow of blood and causes the blood pressure to rise. If a lump of cholesterol breaks off it could block an artery, causing the artery to burst.

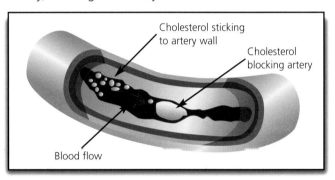

Cholesterol sticking to artery wall
Cholesterol blocking artery
Blood flow

If an artery bursts in the brain it can cause a stroke. If it bursts in a coronary artery, it can cause heart disease.

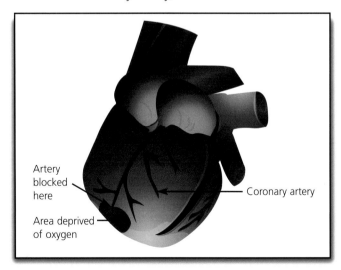

Artery blocked here
Coronary artery
Area deprived of oxygen

Many processed foods contain a lot of sugar, fat and salt. Large quantities of processed foods are consumed because they are 'fast foods', i.e. they are quick and easy to prepare. They are also promoted in the media, which encourages many people to consume them.

Food Additives

Food Additives

Food additives are used to improve the taste and appearance of food, and to increase its shelf-life. You need to know…
- the functions of additives
- examples of different types of additives
- the advantages and disadvantages of using additives.

Food Additives

Food additives are substances that are added to food to improve the taste and appearance and increase the shelf-life. There are different types of additives:
- colourings
- preservatives
- antioxidants
- emulsifiers, stabilisers and thickeners
- flavourings
- flavour enhancers
- sweeteners.

All legal additives (except flavourings) have an 'E' number. Each type of additive begins with a different number.

Colourings (E100s)

Colourings are used to replace the natural colour that is lost during food processing or storage, or to make products a consistent colour. Some examples are listed below:

Colouring	Source	Used In
Caramel, E150a (brown)	• Sugar	• Gravy • Soft drinks
Carotene, E160a (orange or yellow)	• Carrots • Green vegetables • Tomatoes	• Butter • Margarine • Soft drinks
Curcumin, E100 (orange–yellow)	• The roots of the turmeric plant	• Curry • Processed foods

Preservatives (E200s)

Preservatives stop mould or bacteria growing. They keep food fresh for longer by stopping it 'going off'. Most food that has a long shelf-life is likely to include preservatives, unless another method of preserving has been used, e.g. freezing, canning or drying. Some examples are listed below:

Preservative	Used In
Sulfur dioxide, E220	• Dried fruit, e.g. apricots
Benzoic acid, E210	• Fruit yoghurt • Jam • Pickles • Sauces • Soft drinks
Sodium nitrite, E250	• 'Cured' meats, e.g. bacon, corned beef, ham, salami
Sorbic acid, E200	• Bakery products • Dairy products • Fish • Low-fat spreads • Soft drinks

Antioxidants (E300s)

Antioxidants may be used in any food that contains fats or oils – from meat pies to mayonnaise. Antioxidants make foods last longer by helping to stop the fats and oils from oxidising (combining with oxygen in the air). Oxidation makes food become rancid, lose colour and taste 'off'.

Antioxidant	Used In
Vitamin C (ascorbic acid), E300	• Beer (to increase shelf-life) • Cured meat (to help maintain colour) • Fruit juice (to prevent discolouration) • Processed foods (to replace vitamin C lost during processing)

Food Additives

Emulsifiers, Stabilisers and Thickeners (E400s)

Emulsifiers help mix together ingredients that would normally separate, for example, oil and water.

Stabilisers prevent a mixture of ingredients, for example, oil and water, from separating again.

Thickeners are added to help give body to food, for example, adding flour to thicken a sauce.

Additive Type	Example	Used In
Emulsifier	• Egg yolk • Mustard • Lecithin	• Mayonnaise • Salad dressings
Stabiliser	• Corn starch • Potato starch	• Ice creams • Salad dressings • Sauces
Thickener	• Corn starch • Potato starch	• Jams • Low-fat spreads • Puddings • Sauces • Soups

Flavourings

Flavourings are added to foods in very small amounts to give the food a particular taste or smell. Flavourings do not have E numbers because they are controlled by different laws from other food additives.

Flavouring	Used In
Peppermint	• Chewing gum • Chocolate • Tea
Lemon	• Sweets • Cakes • Biscuits • Soft drinks
Vanilla	• Ice cream • Cakes • Yoghurt
Smoke	• Smoked meats • Smoked fish

Flavour Enhancers (E600s)

Flavour enhancers are used to bring out the flavour in a wide range of savoury snacks, ready meals and sweet foods without adding a flavour of their own.

Flavour Enhancer	Used In
Monosodium glutamate (MSG), E621	• Processed foods, e.g. soups, sauces, sausages
Salt (does not have an E number)	• Crisps • Ready meals • Tinned vegetables

Sweeteners (E900s)

Sweeteners are much sweeter than sugar (sucrose) and so are only used in tiny amounts. They are used in diet drinks and in low-calorie or sugar-free foods and sweets.

Sweetener	Used In
Aspartame, E951 (200 times sweeter than sucrose)	• Chewing gum • Sugar-free drinks
Sucralose, E955 (modified sucrose, 600 times sweeter than sucrose)	• Sugar-free sweets • Medicines • Ketchup

Disadvantages of Using Additives

Although colourings can be used to make food look more appealing, some people think that adding colours is unnecessary and misleading. Some food colourings have also been associated with health risks. For example, tartrazine (E102), a synthetic yellow dye, may cause some people to have an allergic reaction, and is often blamed for hyperactivity in children.

Some preservatives are toxic and are linked to health risks. For example, sodium nitrite (E250), may be potentially carcinogenic (cancer-causing), and benzoic acid (E210) can cause some people to develop an allergic rash.

Food Science

Food Labelling and Food Testing

Food labels contain information about the nutrients and energy values of foods. You need to be able to…

- interpret food labels
- carry out qualitative and quantitative tests on food samples
- explain the long-term effects of eating certain foods.

Food Labels

Foods generally contain more than one nutrient, so a food label includes detailed information in order to tell the consumer exactly what the food contains.

The label needs to show certain information:

- **Nutritional information** – shows the energy value of the food by mass, as well as the amount of each type of nutrient (see diagram A).
- **Ingredients** – must all be listed, in order of their mass, with the largest first. Food additives must be included either by name or by E number. The job an additive does – such as adding colour or acting as a preservative – is also shown (see diagram A).
- A **date mark**:
  - A **use by date** is used on highly perishable foods, for example, meat, milk and cream. It is illegal to sell the food after this date (see diagram B).
  - A **best before date** is used on less perishable foods, for example, cereals, biscuits and canned food. The food should not be eaten after this date because it may not be safe to eat (see diagram C).
- **Storage instructions** tell you how to store the product in order to keep it in the best condition, for example, 'in a cool and dry place', 'once opened keep refrigerated', 'keep frozen' (see diagram D).

TOMATO SOUP

NUTRITION INFORMATION

Typical Values	Per 100g
Energy	182kJ
Protein	0.8g
Carbohydrates	6.0g
Fat	1.8g
Fibre	0.6g
Sodium	0.3g

INGREDIENTS
Tomatoes (81%), Water, Vegetable Oil, Sugar, Modified Cornflour, Salt, Dried Skimmed Milk, Cream, Spice Extracts, E120 (Colour), E200 (Preservative) Herbs, E330 Citric Acid (Antioxidant).

USE BY: 27 OCT 07

PASTEURISED MILK

BEST BEFORE END 29 DECEMBER 2009

TOMATO SOUP

VEGETABLE PIE

How to store…
Food Freezer †✹✹✹✹	}	Until Best
'Star' marked †✹✹✹	}	Before Date
Frozen Food ✹✹		1 Month
Compartments ✹		1 Week

† Should be -18°C or colder

Eat on day of purchase, if not kept frozen. Do not re-freeze after thawing.

Testing Food

There are regulations governing the information that needs to be included on a food label. In order to ensure that the information is accurate, food analysts can carry out tests on the food to determine its composition. The tests can be either **qualitative** or **quantitative**.

Qualitative Tests

Qualitative tests reveal whether a substance is present in a food. The qualitative tests that food analysts carry out include tests for…

- starch (see p.9)
- reducing sugar (see p.9)
- protein (see p.9)
- fat (see p.10)
- acidity (see below).

Finding the Acidity or Alkalinity of a Food Sample

The acidity or alkalinity (i.e. pH) of a sample of food can be found using universal indicator liquid or paper. The colour produced with the indicator can then be compared to a pH colour chart (see opposite).

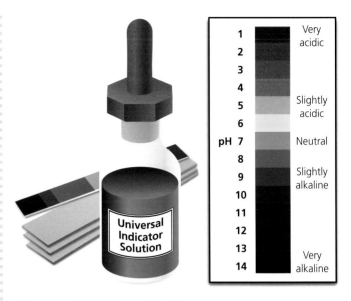

Quantitative Tests

Quantitative tests reveal how much of a substance is present in a food or a food supplement.

Food analysts carry out quantitative tests on food to determine the…

- vitamin C content (see p.12)
- iron content (see p.13)
- moisture / water content (see p.14)
- acidity (see p.20)
- percentage of suspended matter, i.e. fibre (see p.21).

Food Science

Finding the Acidity of a Food Sample

Acidity is a measure of the number of hydrogen ($H^+_{(aq)}$) ions present.

You can find the acidity by carrying out a **titration** to measure how much alkali is needed to neutralise the acid in a fixed volume.

The following method can be used:

1. Measure out $10cm^3$ of the sample (e.g. fruit juice) into a flask.
2. Add a few drops of indicator, for example, phenolphthalein.
3. Carry out a titration to find the volume of sodium hydroxide needed to neutralise the fruit juice (see diagram A). The indicator will remain colourless in acid and will turn pink in alkali. The end point of the titration is when the pink colour first appears in the fruit juice.

It might be difficult to see the end point of the titration because of the colour of the fruit juice. You can use a pH meter to help you find the end point (pH 7) accurately (see diagram B).

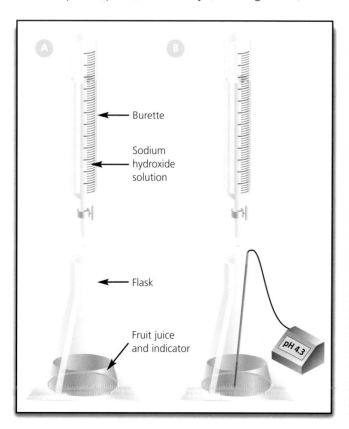

Citric acid is the most common acid in fruit juice. The equation for neutralising citric acid with sodium hydroxide is…

citric acid	+	sodium hydroxide	→	sodium citrate	+	water

Since you only need to know the number of H^+ ions, this equation can be simplified to…

$$H^+_{(aq)} + OH^-_{(aq)} \longrightarrow H_2O_{(l)}$$

The equation shows that 1 mole of H^+ ions is neutralised by 1 mole of OH^- ions. This can be used to produce the following formula:

Concentration of H^+ ions (mol dm^{-3})	X	Volume of acid (dm³)	=	Concentration of NaOH (mol dm^{-3})	X	Volume of NaOH (dm³)

Example

A titration is carried out and $0.06dm^3$ sodium hydroxide, of concentration $1mol\ dm^{-3}$, neutralises $0.02dm^3$ orange juice. Calculate the acidity (or H^+ ion concentration) of the orange juice.

Use the formula…

$$\text{Concentration of } H^+ \text{ ions} \times \text{Volume of acid} = \text{Concentration of NaOH} \times \text{Volume of NaOH}$$

$$\text{Concentration of } H^+ \text{ ions} \times 0.02dm^3 = 1mol\ dm^3 \times 0.06dm^3$$

$$\text{Concentration of } H^+ \text{ ions} = \frac{1 \times 0.06}{0.02}$$

$$= \mathbf{3mol\ dm^{-3}}$$

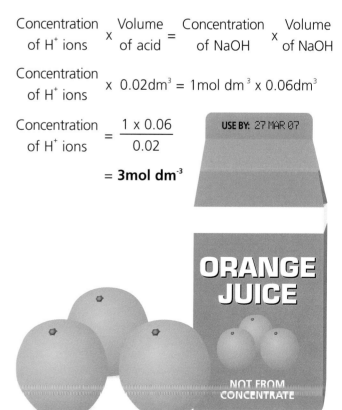

Finding the Percentage of Suspended Matter (Fibre) in a Food Sample by Filtration

The percentage of suspended matter (i.e. fibre, or pulp) contained in a food sample, e.g. fruit juice, can be found using the following method:

1 Find the mass of an empty measuring cylinder.

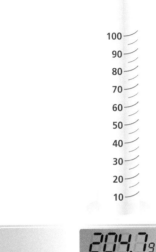
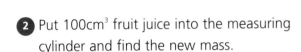

2 Put 100cm³ fruit juice into the measuring cylinder and find the new mass.

Fruit juice

3 Subtract the mass of the measuring cylinder from the total mass to find the mass of 100cm³ fruit juice.

4 Filter the juice.

Residue

Filtrate

5 Find the mass of the filtrate.

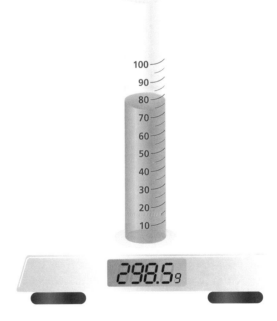

6 Work out the percentage mass of the suspended matter using the following formula:

$$\text{Percentage mass of suspended matter} = \frac{\text{Initial mass of juice} - \text{Mass of filtrate}}{\text{Initial mass of juice}} \times 100$$

Example

100cm³ fruit juice has a mass of 123.7g, and the mass of the filtrate is 93.8g. Find the percentage mass of the suspended matter.

Use the equation…

$$\text{Percentage mass of suspended matter} = \frac{123.7 - 93.8}{123.7} \times 100$$

$$= \textbf{24.2\%}$$

Food Science

Useful Microorganisms in the Production of Food

Certain microorganisms can be used in the production of food and drinks. You need to be able to describe how bacteria, yeast and other fungi are used to make food products like beer, wine, bread, cheese and yoghurt.

Microorganisms

The term **microorganisms** is used to refer to **yeast**, other **fungi**, and **bacteria**.

Microbiologists study microorganisms to find out where and how they grow, what factors affect their growth, and what substances they make.

Microorganisms grow best when they have…
- food
- warmth
- moisture
- optimum pH (usually pH 7)
- oxygen (however, not all microorganisms need oxygen).

Some microorganisms are useful because they can be used in the production of food. For example, yeast is used to make beer and wine (see opposite) and bread (see p.23), and bacteria are used to make yoghurt and cheese (see p.23). However, not all microorganisms are useful; some produce harmful substances called **toxins** (see p.24).

Yeast

Yeast uses **anaerobic respiration** (respiration without oxygen) to release energy from glucose. This process is called **fermentation**.

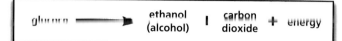

glucose $\longrightarrow$ ethanol (alcohol) + carbon dioxide + energy

Making Beer
Yeast is used in beer making. The stages are:
1. **Malting** – Barley grains are soaked in water and allowed to germinate. Enzymes in the grains break down starch to malt sugar (maltose).
2. **Extracting** – The grain is crushed, then filtered using hot water, to extract a sugary liquid called wort. The wort is boiled with hops to give a bitter flavour and denature any enzymes to stop them working.
3. **Fermentation** – Yeast is added and the mixture is kept between 15°C and 25°C. Enzymes in the yeast change sugars to ethanol and carbon dioxide. The yeast is filtered off and the beer is put into bottles and cans.

Making Wine
Yeast is used in wine making. The stages are:
1. Grapes are crushed and put into a fermentation tank, which is kept at about 30°C.
2. Enzymes in the yeast (which grows on grape skins) convert sugars in the grapes to ethanol.
3. The wine is left in barrels for a few months to mature before bottling.

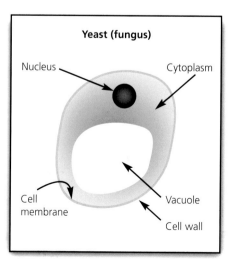

Yeast (fungus)
Nucleus
Cytoplasm
Cell membrane
Vacuole
Cell wall

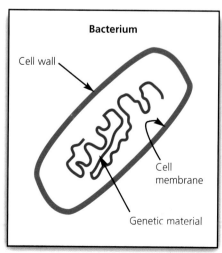

Bacterium
Cell wall
Cell membrane
Genetic material

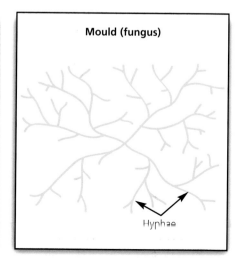

Mould (fungus)
Hyphae

Making Bread

Yeast is used in bread making. The stages are:

1 Yeast, salt, flour and water are mixed to make dough.

2 The dough is left in a warm place (at about 25°C).

3 Amylase enzymes in the yeast change starch in the flour to glucose. Fermentation takes place, releasing carbon dioxide, which makes the dough rise.

4 The dough is baked at about 220°C. The bubbles of carbon dioxide expand and are trapped in the dough, giving the bread a spongy texture. Any ethanol evaporates and enzymes in the yeast are denatured so all reactions stop.

Bacteria

Making Yoghurt

Bacteria are used in the production of yoghurt. The stages are:

1 A starter culture of lactic acid bacteria is added to milk.

2 The milk is warmed to about 40°C.

3 Enzymes in the bacteria change lactose (milk sugar) to lactic acid, making the pH lower, which gives it a sour taste.

4 The acid also makes the milk proteins clot and solidify into yoghurt.

Making Cheese

Bacteria and moulds are used in cheese making. The stages are:

1 Milk is heated or pasteurised to kill any microorganisms which may be present.

2 The milk is cooled to about 30°C and a starter culture of bacteria is added. For blue cheese, a mould is also added.

3 Enzymes in the bacteria change lactose (milk sugar) to lactic acid.

4 Rennet, which contains enzymes, is stirred into the milk. The enzymes make the milk clot into lumps (called curds) leaving a watery liquid (called whey).

5 The whey is drained off, leaving the solid curd.

6 Salt is added to the curds to make cheese, which is then shaped and left to ripen.

Beer and Wine

Bread

Yoghurt

Cheese

Food Science

Microorganisms and Food Safety

Harmful microorganisms can cause food poisoning. You need to know…

- examples of bacteria that can cause food poisoning
- the symptoms of food poisoning
- the optimum conditions for the growth of bacteria
- examples of techniques for stopping or slowing down the growth of bacteria
- the meaning of aseptic technique
- how to keep food preparation areas free from bacteria
- how to determine the levels of bacteria present in food samples.

Harmful Microorganisms

Food poisoning is caused when microorganisms (usually bacteria) contaminate food and produce **toxins** when they grow. The **symptoms** of food poisoning may include fever, stomach pains, vomiting, diarrhoea and headaches. The table below shows different ways in which you can be infected by bacteria.

Bacterium	How You Can Be Infected
Campylobacter	• Eating undercooked poultry and red meat • Drinking unpasteurised milk • Drinking untreated water
E. coli (most strains are harmless)	• Eating undercooked minced beef • Drinking unpasteurised milk • By direct contact with infected animals or people • By contact with animal faeces
Salmonella	• Eating undercooked red meat, poultry and eggs, and raw egg products • Drinking unpasteurised milk • By direct contact with infected people

Investigating Microorganisms

Microorganisms can be found everywhere, for example, in the air, in water, on your hands, on tables.

When investigating microorganisms you need to use **aseptic (sterile) technique** in order to prevent…

- microorganisms from the environment contaminating the experiment
- microorganisms from the experiment contaminating the environment.

Aseptic technique includes…

- using equipment and culture media that have been sterilised, e.g. in an autoclave
- working in a draught-free area
- following standard procedures, e.g. labelling petri dishes on the bottom, flaming loops, and cleaning benches with disinfectant after use
- incubating cultures in secured containers. (When sticking down the lid of a petri dish, only use three or four pieces of tape; sealing the dish completely may allow the growth of harmful anaerobic bacteria.)
- incubating petri dishes at a maximum temperature of 25°C to prevent the growth of harmful pathogens that grow at body temperature (37°C).

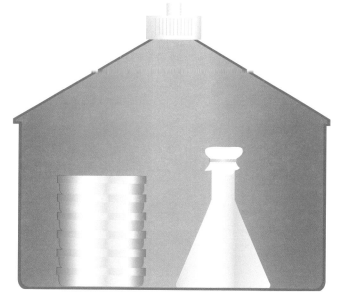

Autoclave – used to sterilise equipment at high temperature and pressure

When carrying out these investigations, remember to use aseptic techniques.

Finding Where Bacteria Grow

1 Dip a sterile cotton bud in sterile water.

2 Streak the cotton bud over the surface of the agar of a sterile petri dish. Label this dish 'control' and seal with sticky tape.

3 Use another sterile cotton bud to wipe the surface of a bench.

4 Streak the cotton bud over the surface of the agar of a sterile petri dish. Label the dish and seal with sticky tape.

5 Repeat steps 3 and 4, collecting samples from a door handle, a coin and the floor.

6 Incubate the petri dishes upside down in a warm place for a few days. Then compare the number of colonies of bacteria on each dish. You should not find any colonies of bacteria or mould growing on the control petri dish.

Finding the Number of Bacteria in a Food Sample

1 For liquids like milk and yoghurt, mix $1cm^3$ of the sample with $9cm^3$ sterile water in a test tube to make a 10% solution. Label the test tube F1. For solid samples, mix a small amount of the sample with sufficient water to produce a 10% solution, for example, 10g made up to $100cm^3$ with water. You can use a glass rod to gently crush the food and mix it with the water. (In an industrial laboratory, the food would be mixed in a sterile blender.)

2 Prepare a dilution series of test tubes by measuring $9cm^3$ water into each test tube. Then transfer $1cm^3$ of the sample mixture from tube F1 into tube F2 and mix thoroughly.

Then transfer $1cm^3$ from tube F2 into tube F3 and mix thoroughly. Continue the process to produce a dilution series (as below).

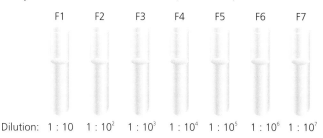

Dilution: 1 : 10 $1 : 10^2$ $1 : 10^3$ $1 : 10^4$ $1 : 10^5$ $1 : 10^6$ $1 : 10^7$

3 Place $1cm^3$ of F2, F3, F4, F5, F6 and F7 in separate labelled petri dishes. Pour melted agar into each dish, and swirl gently to mix the sample and agar.

4 Allow the agar to set. Tape the lids to the dishes and turn them upside down.

5 Incubate the dishes at 25°C for a few days.

6 Choose a dish that has a reasonable number of colonies (i.e. between 20 and 100) and count the number of colonies in it. Each colony will have grown from a single cell, so you can use the number of colonies to calculate the number of bacteria per litre or gram of food, using this equation:

$$\text{Number of bacteria / cm}^3 = \text{Number of colonies} \times \text{Dilution of sample}$$

Example

Calculate the number of bacteria in a food sample if the diagram below represents the bacteria found in petri dish F6.

There are 24 colonies on the petri dish. Use the formula…

$$\text{Number of bacteria / cm}^3 = \text{Number of colonies} \times \text{Dilution of sample}$$

$$= 24 \times 10^6$$

$$= \mathbf{2.4 \times 10^7} \text{ or } \mathbf{24\,000\,000 \text{ colonies}}$$

Food Science

Food Hygiene

There are microorganisms on us and all around us. Food hygiene is about reducing the risk of being harmed by what we eat or drink.

Food safety guidelines and regulations are followed by the people who are responsible for checking that food is handled and stored correctly:

- **Hygiene and quality control staff** carry out this task in industry.
- **Public health inspectors** are responsible for checking public places, e.g. shops and restaurants.

Food Safety Guidelines

Personal Hygiene

- Always wash your hands, or use antiseptic soap or wipes, to remove bacteria before handling food. (**Antiseptics** are chemicals which kill microorganisms, and are safe to use on human skin.)
- Do not cough or sneeze over food.
- Cover any cuts with a clean plaster.
- Tie your hair back.
- Wear a clean apron.

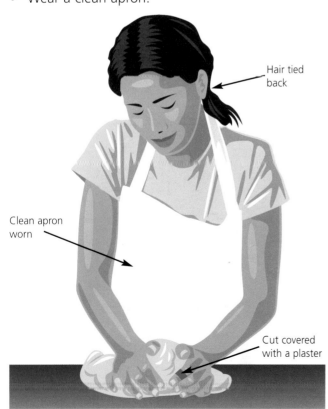

Hair tied back

Clean apron worn

Cut covered with a plaster

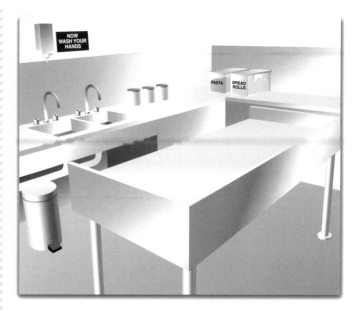

Kitchen Hygiene

Disinfectants are chemicals which kill microorganisms. They contain concentrated germicides which are too strong to be used on human skin, but can be used to clean floors, work surfaces and table tops.

Detergents are used in soaps and washing-up liquids. They clean by breaking down oil and fats into tiny droplets which then mix with water.

Utensils should be washed thoroughly before and after dealing with raw foods in order to prevent cooked foods from becoming contaminated with microorganisms.

In the food industry, equipment is **sterilised** by using steam to heat it to very high temperatures so that all microorganisms are killed (see autoclave, p.24).

Waste should be disposed of carefully. All waste bins should have a lid to reduce the chance of the microorganisms that grow on waste food coming into contact with food or utensils. Bins should be emptied regularly.

Pests

Simple steps can be taken to prevent pests from coming into contact with food, for example...

- cover food to prevent insects from landing on it
- store food in metal or plastic containers to prevent mice and rats from contaminating it
- never store food on the floor.

Storing Food

The growth of bacteria that may be present in food can be slowed down, or stopped completely, by using one of the following methods:

Refrigeration keeps food at about 4°C. At this temperature, microorganisms only grow slowly.

Freezing stores food at about -20°C. This temperature is too low for enzymes to work. However, bacteria are not killed, so when the food is thawed they will start to grow. This is why food needs to be cooked properly after it has been frozen.

Heating food to a high temperature kills bacteria. Food needs to be cooked for long enough at the right temperature to kill bacteria:

- Tinned foods are heated and then sealed. This prevents air from getting in so microorganisms are unable to grow.
- Milk is **pasteurised** by heating it to 71°C for 15 seconds, followed by rapid cooling. This kills most microorganisms, but if the milk is left in a warm place any microorganisms present soon start to grow, turning the milk sour.
- **UHT** (ultra high temperature) milk is heated to 132°C for 2 seconds, which kills all microorganisms.

Drying removes water from food so bacteria cannot grow. Freeze-drying is the process of freezing food and then placing it in a vacuum under pressure. On heating, any ice changes to a vapour, leaving the food dry.

Salting food (i.e. storing it in a salt solution) reduces the amount of water present in food because water moves out of the food into the salt solution by **osmosis**. The salt also dehydrates any microorganisms by drawing water out of them by osmosis.

Osmosis is the movement of water from a dilute to a more concentrated solution through a partially permeable membrane (see diagram below). In other words, water diffuses from where it is in high concentration to where it is in low concentration.

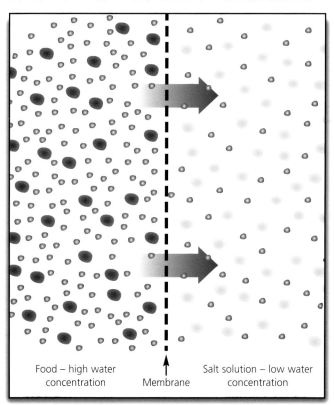

Food – high water concentration   Membrane   Salt solution – low water concentration

Preserving with sugar (for example, as jam) prevents microorganisms from growing because they become dehydrated: the water is drawn out of them by osmosis into the concentrated sugar syrup.

Pickling is when food is stored in vinegar, which is acidic (pH 3–4). The enzymes in microorganisms are denatured so they are unable to grow.

Food Science

Organic and Intensive Farming

Food can be produced by either intensive or organic farming. You need to know…

- about the minerals that plants need for healthy growth
- that intensive farming increases yields by using artificial fertilisers, pesticides, herbicides and fungicides, and increases meat production by using controlled environments
- that organic farming uses natural fertilisers and alternative methods of pest control, and keeps animals under more natural conditions
- the advantages and disadvantages of organic and intensive farming, so you can compare them.

Producing Food

Green plants are the original source of all our food. They make their own food by a process called **photosynthesis**. Their leaves contain **chlorophyll**, which traps light energy and uses it to make carbohydrates. Photosynthesis can be represented by the following equation:

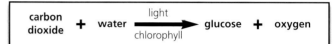

$$ \text{carbon dioxide} + \text{water} \xrightarrow[\text{chlorophyll}]{\text{light}} \text{glucose} + \text{oxygen} $$

To help plants grow well and produce a high yield of grain, fruit or vegetables, they need…

- water
- carbon dioxide
- light
- warmth
- minerals.

Essential Minerals

The table below shows the function of some minerals needed by plants and the effects of a shortage:

Nitrates (NO_3^-)	Phosphates (PO_4^-)	Potassium (K^+)	Magnesium (Mg^{2+})
Function Needed to make amino acids and proteins to enable the growth of shoots and leaves.	**Functions** Needed for photosynthesis and respiration, and to make proteins and DNA.	**Functions** Helps enzymes involved in photosynthesis and respiration; needed to make flowers and fruits.	**Function** Needed to make chlorophyll.
Effects of Shortage Stunted growth and yellow leaves.	**Effects of Shortage** Poor root growth and small, purple leaves.	**Effect of Shortage** Yellow leaves with dead spots.	**Effect of Shortage** Yellow patches on leaves.

Increasing Food Production

Farmers try to produce as much food as possible by making the best use of their land, plants and animals. There are two approaches to farming – **intensive** and **organic** – which use different techniques.

Farming Plants

As plants grow, they absorb minerals from the soil through their roots. They absorb…

* nitrogen (N) as nitrates or ammonium salts
* phosphorus (P) as phosphates
* potassium (K) as potassium salts
* magnesium (Mg) as magnesium salts.

These minerals can be replaced by adding fertilisers to the soil. There are two kinds of fertiliser:

* **Artificial fertilisers** are made in large chemical plants and usually contain the elements nitrogen, phosphorus and potassium. They are used in intensive farming.
* **Natural fertilisers**, like **manure** and seaweed, are used in organic farming.

Some advantages and disadvantages of each type of fertiliser are listed below:

Type of Fertiliser	Advantages	Disadvantages
Artificial Fertiliser (used in intensive farming)	• Cheap • Ample supplies • Easy to spread • Easy to control quantities • Easy to add different nutrients in required quantities	• Finite resources are being used up • Extracting the chemicals may affect the environment • Concentrated, so too much may be added • Can lead to eutrophication of rivers and lakes
Organic Fertiliser (used in organic farming)	• Does not use up finite resources • Does not harm the environment • Materials are recycled • Improves soil texture	• Plants grow more slowly than if artificial fertilisers are used • Lower yield • Products are more expensive

Controlling Pests and Diseases

Pests are the insects, weeds, fungi, viruses, rodents, etc. that prevent plants from growing, and reduce crop yields. The pests are reduced or eliminated in different ways in intensive and organic farming.

Intensive Farming

Manufactured chemicals called **pesticides** are used to get rid of pests in intensive farming:

- Insects, for example, aphids and caterpillars, are killed using **insecticides**.
- **Weeds** are plants that grow where they are not wanted, and compete with crops for nutrients, light and water. They can be killed using **herbicides**.
- Fungi, e.g, mildew, are killed using **fungicides**.

Organic Farming

A range of methods are used to control the numbers of pests.

Insects can be controlled by…
- **biological control** – natural predators such as birds, bats, beetles, parasitic wasps, ladybirds and lacewings feed on insect pests
- **encouraging biodiversity** – hedges and 'beetle banks' (piles of branches left to decay naturally) are planted to provide a habitat for predators of pest species
- **crop rotation** – different types of crop are grown in a field each year. This causes a break in the life cycle of the pest by removing the 'host' crop for a few years
- selective breeding – new varieties of plants can be obtained which are more resistant to diseases and pests
- **organic pesticides** – naturally occurring compounds, for example, liquid soap, can be used to control aphids. Rotenone (a natural extract from plants) can only be used as a last resort as it can have harmful effects on beneficial insects as well as pests.

Weeds can be controlled by…
- **using mulches, compost or bark** – covers the soil between plants, which prevents growth
- **weeding** – using machines, for example, a hoe, or by hand.

Fungi can be controlled by using…
- **selective breeding** – obtaining new varieties of plants that are more resistant to diseases
- **natural (organic) fungicides** – sulfur or copper salts can be used to control fungal diseases, for example, potato blight.

Method of Pest Control	Advantages	Disadvantages
Pesticides (used in intensive farming)	• Not labour intensive • Food can be sold more cheaply	• Use up finite resources (e.g. oil) in manufacture • Insecticides are not selective, so they kill helpful insects as well as pests
Biological Controls (used in organic farming)	• Do not use up finite resources • Less chance of pesticide residues on food • Pests cannot become resistant to the predators	• Labour intensive • Breeding resistant plants takes many years • Products are more expensive • Pests are not eliminated; numbers are just reduced

Farming Animals

Intensive farming increases food production by using controlled environments so that animals, for example, chickens, pigs and fish, grow as fast as possible. This is done by...

- limiting the animals' movement, so less energy is wasted and they grow more quickly
- keeping animals warm, so not as much of their energy is needed to produce heat
- using antibiotics to reduce the spread of disease
- feeding the animals a high-protein diet with additives
- excluding predators.

Organic farming is more concerned with the animals' welfare. Animals are kept under more natural conditions, i.e. they can move around freely. However, because more energy is used for movement and keeping warm, less energy is available for growth.

Organically raised animals, for example, free-range chickens, have a large area to move around in, rather than being kept in a cage like a battery hen. As a result, free-range chickens use more energy to move about and keep warm, so less energy is available to produce eggs, and for growth. This is why they do not produce as many eggs as battery hens.

Method of Rearing Animals	Advantages	Disadvantages
Controlled Conditions (used in intensive farming)	• Cheaper food because animals grow more quickly	• Some people consider these methods to be cruel to animals
Natural Conditions (used in organic farming)	• No chance of antibiotic residues or additives in food • More humane to animals	• Animals grow more slowly • Products are more expensive

Farming Animals Intensively

Farming Animals Organically

Forensic Science

Collecting Evidence from the Crime Scene

Forensic investigation begins by observing and recording materials found at the crime scene. You need to know how to…

- avoid the contamination of evidence
- measure, record, collect and label different types of samples
- take appropriate samples from large quantities of materials
- make and take a permanent record of a mark or an impression
- reveal and lift a fingerprint
- recognise three types of fingerprint patterns
- evaluate the validity and reliability of evidence.

Forensic Science

Scientific techniques are used to identify and match samples from crime scenes to known substances and objects. This branch of science is known as **forensic science**.

Although it is mainly used to help the police to investigate crimes, forensic methods can also be used to…

- find the cause of an industrial accident
- study and date archaeological specimens
- establish whether or not people are related.

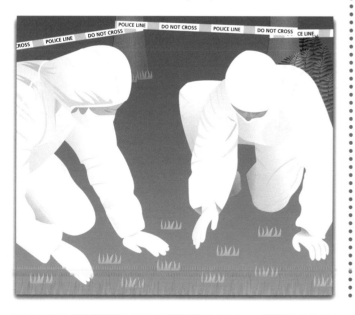

Forensic Science at a Crime Scene

Evidence at a **crime scene** must be prevented from becoming **contaminated**, for example, with any substances that were not present when the crime took place, as this could affect the results of forensic tests. Contamination of evidence can be prevented by…

- restricting access, for example, by using tape barriers to prevent unauthorised entry
- wearing protective clothing, for example, body suit, hood, gloves, footwear covers, etc.
- using appropriate methods of sampling, storage and recording.

Recording Evidence

Forensic work starts with the careful **observation** and **recording** of materials found at a crime scene.

Evidence can be recorded by…

- writing a description of the crime scene
- drawing diagrams
- shooting videos
- using photography, i.e. wide-angle views of the crime scene and then close-up shots of evidence. Each photo must include a **scale** so the size of the object can be measured
- taking witness statements, which may include a description of the suspect's sex, height, weight, hair colour, eye colour, clothing, and any distinguishing physical features, e.g. scars, moles or tattoos.

After talking to witnesses, a representation of a suspect's face could be created by…

- an artist drawing from a witness's description
- a witness using an **identikit database**.

An identikit database contains thousands of images of facial features such as eyes, chins, noses, mouths and hair. The witness chooses the features that resemble those of the suspect. The images can then be put together to make an identikit image, to show a likeness of the suspect. Computer imaging blurs the edges to produce an image similar to a photograph.

Accuracy and Reliability of Evidence

Samples, marks and impressions left at the crime scene are analysed (see p.41–52) and compared with samples from a suspect, for example, hair, blood, DNA, fingerprints, tools, car tyres and shoe soles. The results of the comparisons could eliminate suspects from police inquiries, or indicate that further investigation is needed.

The evidence may need to be used in a court of law, so it needs to be **accurate** and **reliable** in order for it to be considered **valid**.

It is very important that correct sampling procedures are followed; an inappropriate collection or sampling technique may lead to uncertainty about the validity and reliability of evidence.

Accuracy refers to how close a measurement is to the actual value. Accuracy depends on the precision of a measuring instrument.

For example, if you want to measure out $5cm^3$ water, you could use a $25cm^3$ measuring cylinder or a $10cm^3$ syringe. Because the markings are further apart on the syringe, you can measure out the water more precisely.

Reliability refers to the confidence you have in the data you have collected, i.e. the likelihood that the same results would be obtained if the analysis were to be repeated again and again.

Taking Samples

Samples need to be carefully collected and labelled without introducing any **contamination**, as this would lead to uncertainty about the **validity** of the evidence.

When collecting evidence, you need to take sufficient samples to be able to **repeat** the analysis two to four times, if necessary. Repeating an analysis enables you to check the accuracy of the analysis. (You may have made an error on one or more of the tests, which could have affected the results.)

Tests are usually carried out on small samples, but if there is a large quantity of material, you need to consider the following questions:
- How much material is needed for one test?
- How many tests are needed in order to get a reliable result?
- Is the composition of the material **homogenous** (the same throughout)? If you are not sure then you should take samples from different places and mix them together thoroughly and then analyse the mixture.

Example

You have been asked to check whether a number of bags labelled 'flour' actually contain flour, not banned substances. How would you do this?

To check the flour, you should take several samples from each bag, then mix all the samples together until the mixture is homogenous. Samples of this mixture should then be analysed several times.

Forensic Science

Collecting Evidence

Items found at the crime scene need to be collected and taken away as evidence.

Before moving a piece of evidence or a sample, forensic investigators need to...
- photograph it with a scale to show its size
- record a description of where it was found.

Types of Evidence

There are many types of evidence that may need to be collected at a crime scene. The table below lists some types of evidence and how they should be collected:

Item	Example	Method of Collection
Large article	Any large items found at a crime scene, e.g... • clothing • weapons • anything that may have fingerprints on	• Gloved hand
Fragments of glass or plastic	• Small pieces	• Tweezers • Sticky tape
	• Larger pieces	• Gloved hand
Fibres	• Hair • Textiles	• Gloved hand • Tweezers • Sticky tape
Soil	From the ground	• Scalpel

Large pieces of broken glass or plastic fragments should be wrapped securely in paper or cardboard and then placed inside a cardboard box to prevent further damage.

Samples / evidence should be placed in separate paper envelopes and then inside labelled evidence envelopes, which should be sealed.

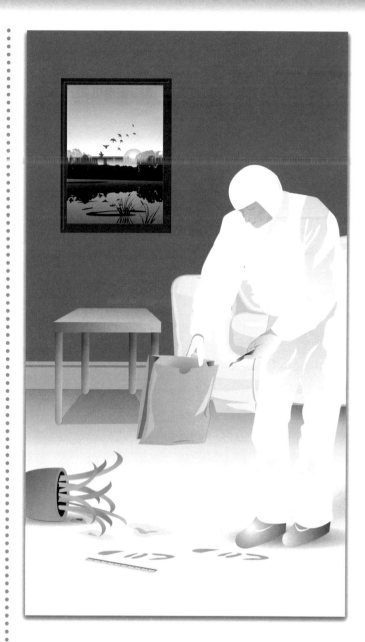

Fingerprints

Fingerprint evidence may be:
- **Visible** – left by the transfer of blood, paint or powder on a surface. They can be seen by the naked eye, and can therefore be photographed.
- **Moulded** – formed as an impression in something soft like soap, putty or candle wax. They can be seen by the naked eye, and can therefore be photographed.
- **Latent** – left by the transfer of sweat and natural oils from the fingers onto a smooth surface. They are not visible to the naked eye and can be lifted in different ways, depending on the surface.

Collecting Fingerprint Evidence

Fingerprints may be present on a range of surfaces.

The method used to reveal and lift a fingerprint depends on the type of surface it has been left on.

Non-Porous Surfaces

Fingerprints on surfaces such as glossy paper, paint, glass or metal are revealed using powders.

The area is dusted with a suitable powder, e.g. black carbon powder, magnetic (iron) powder or grey aluminium powder. The revealed print is then photographed. Sticky tape is used to lift the print and stick it to a fingerprint card of a contrasting colour to the powder (see diagram A).

Porous Surfaces

Fingerprints on surfaces such as paper, cloth and wood are revealed using different chemicals:

- **Ninhydrin** (a fluorescent developer) is sprayed onto the surface. It reacts with amino acids from sweat and causes the prints to fluoresce (give out light) under a laser light.
- **Iodine crystals** vaporise and react with oils in the fingerprint (see diagram B). Tape is stuck over the print to stop the iodine vaporising again.
- **Silver nitrate solution** ($AgNO_3$) is painted onto the surface and dried in the dark. The silver nitrate reacts with chlorides (Cl^-) from sweat to produce silver chloride ($AgCl$) which turns dark grey when exposed to light. Under a bright lamp, the fingerprints appear and can be photographed.

Porous and Non-Porous Surfaces

Fingerprints on surfaces such as plastic bags, car interiors or even human bodies are revealed using superglue.

When superglue is heated, it gives off a vapour containing cyanoacrylates which react with the amino acids, fats and proteins left behind by human touch, forming a plastic mould of the print (see diagram C). The prints can then be dusted with powder to make them more visible for photographing.

A

glass 2
19/02/2007

B

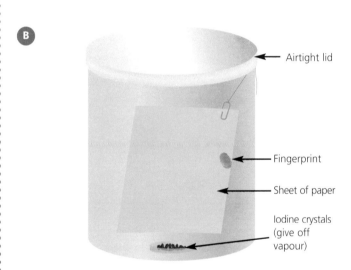

Airtight lid

Fingerprint

Sheet of paper

Iodine crystals (give off vapour)

C

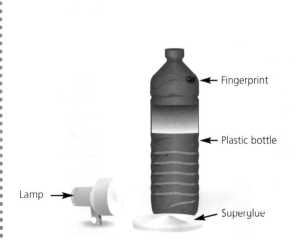

Airtight container

Fingerprint

Plastic bottle

Lamp

Superglue

Forensic Science

Blood

If blood is found at a crime scene, the blood stained areas should be photographed with a scale alongside.

The length and width of any blood spats should then be measured (see diagram A).

Blood samples can be collected by…
- scraping them into a sterile container, using a scalpel
- lifting them, using sterile cotton buds which are then placed in a sterile container or used to make smear slides
- removing them, using a small amount of distilled water, tweezers and a sterile cloth square, which is then placed in a sterile container.

Impressions

Impressions that may be found at a crime scene include tyre tracks, footprints, bite marks in food, and scratches in metal.

The impression should be photographed with a suitable scale next to it.

Casts of larger impressions, e.g. tyre tracks or footprints, can be made using this procedure:
1. Around the impression, place a ring made from plasticine, or cardboard held with a paperclip.
2. Mix water and plaster of Paris in a plastic bag until it is the consistency of thick cream.
3. Pour the mixture into the impression and leave to dry (see diagram B).

Casts of smaller impressions, e.g. scratches on metal, can be made using this procedure:
1. Make a ring around the mark(s) with a strip of plasticine.
2. Make a mixture of sulfur and carbon powder (8 : 2). Heat it in a sand bath (to prevent the sulfur vapour catching fire) until the mixture melts.
3. Pour the mixture into the plasticine ring (see diagram C). Leave to cool and set.

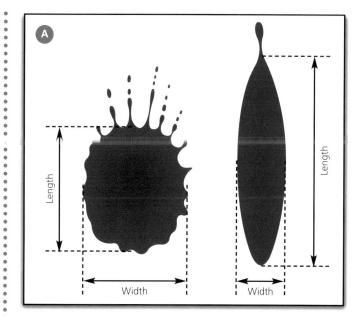

Diagram A — Length and Width

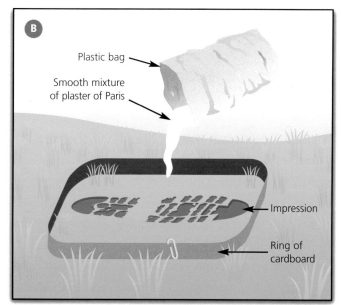

B
Plastic bag
Smooth mixture of plaster of Paris
Impression
Ring of cardboard

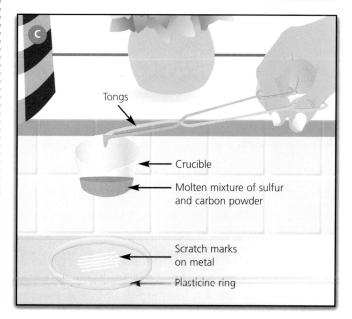

C
Tongs
Crucible
Molten mixture of sulfur and carbon powder
Scratch marks on metal
Plasticine ring

Analysing Evidence from the Crime Scene

Forensic scientists carry out many tests to determine which substances are present in a sample. You need to know…

- about the structure and properties of ionic and covalent compounds
- how to detect the presence of different ions and substances in a sample
- how chromatography can be used to separate and compare coloured samples
- about the use of different types of microscopes
- how to describe distinctive features of soil, hair, fibres, seeds, pollen grains and bullets
- about the composition of blood, and blood groups
- about DNA and DNA profiling
- how light is refracted and how the refractive index can be found.

Analysing Evidence

Analytical chemists carry out two types of test:
- **Qualitative** analysis determines *which* compounds are present.
- **Quantitative** analysis determines *how much* of each compound is present.

Compounds can be identified using **chemical** and / or **physical** properties such as solubility, melting point and boiling point.

The properties of a compound depend upon…
- the elements that are present
- the type of bonding that exists between the elements – ionic or covalent.

Elements

An **element** is a pure substance that cannot be broken down into simpler chemical substances; it contains only one type of atom. About 90 elements occur naturally on Earth.

Each element has its own name and chemical symbol, and unique…
- **physical** properties – i.e. density, electrical conductivity, melting point and boiling point
- **chemical** properties – i.e. reactions with water, oxygen and acids.

The atoms of an element have a **nucleus** that contains **protons** and **neutrons**. The nucleus is surrounded by **electrons**, which are arranged in **energy levels** or **shells**.

For example, sodium has 11 protons, 12 neutrons and 11 electrons.

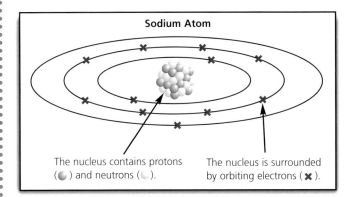

Sodium Atom

The nucleus contains protons ( ) and neutrons ( ).

The nucleus is surrounded by orbiting electrons (✘).

Atoms have no overall charge because each atom contains the same number of protons (which are positively charged) and electrons (which are negatively charged). Neutrons have no charge.

Atomic Number

The number of protons in an atom is called the **proton number** or **atomic number**.

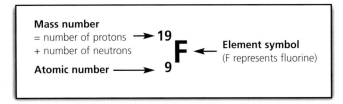

Mass number
= number of protons
+ number of neutrons → 19

Atomic number → 9

$^{19}_{9}\text{F}$ ← Element symbol (F represents fluorine)

Some other element symbols are shown below:

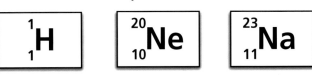

$^{1}_{1}\text{H}$ $^{20}_{10}\text{Ne}$ $^{23}_{11}\text{Na}$

- The atomic number of hydrogen is 1.
- The atomic number of neon is 10.
- The atomic number of sodium is 11.

Forensic Science

The Periodic Table

The periodic table is a way of arranging the elements in order of atomic number. Elements with similar properties are put in the same group.

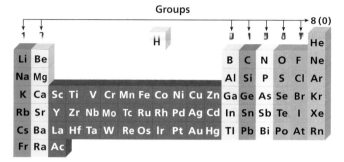

Groups

Electron Configuration

The electrons in an atom are arranged around the nucleus in **shells** or **energy levels**. The first shell can only contain a maximum of 2 electrons. The shells after this can each hold a maximum of 8 electrons.

The electron configuration of an atom is written as, for example, 2.8. which means there are 2 electrons in the first shell and 8 electrons in the second shell. Electron configuration can also be represented in a diagram:

Lithium, Li Atomic number: 3 Electron configuration: 2.1	
Oxygen, O Atomic number: 8 Electron configuration: 2.6	
Neon, Ne Atomic number: 10 Electron configuration: 2.8	

The elements in a **group** have similar properties because they have the same number of electrons in their outer electron shell, so…

- all the elements in Group 1 have 1 electron in their outer electron shell
- all the elements in Group 7 have 7 electrons in their outer electron shell
- all the elements in Group 8 (0) have a full outer shell of electrons (i.e. 8 electrons in their outer shell).

Bonding

The bonds between the atoms of elements in a compound can be **ionic** or **covalent**.

Ionic Bonding

Ionic bonding occurs between a **metal** atom and a **non-metal** atom. It involves a **transfer** of electrons from one atom to another to form electrically charged **ions**:

- Atoms which **lose** electrons have fewer electrons than protons, and become **positively** charged ions.
- Atoms which **gain** electrons have more electrons than protons, and become **negatively** charged ions.

The ions formed have the electronic structure of a Group 8 (0) element, i.e. they have a full outer shell of electrons.

The compounds formed do not have a charge because the charge on the positive ion(s) is equal to the charge on the negative ion(s).

Example 1 – Sodium Chloride

The sodium atom (Na) has 1 electron in its outer shell which is transferred to the chlorine atom (Cl). They now both have 8 electrons in their outer shells. The atoms are now ions (Na^+ and Cl^-) and the compound formed is sodium chloride (NaCl).

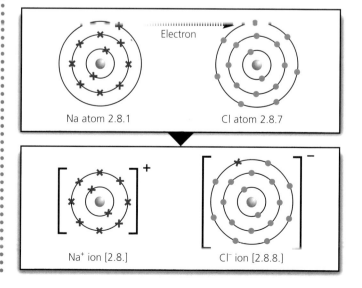

Example 2 – Calcium Chloride

calcium + chlorine ⟶ calcium chloride

The calcium atom (Ca) has 2 electrons in its outer shell. The chlorine atom (Cl) only needs 1 electron to fill its outer shell, therefore 2 chlorine atoms are needed. When the electrons are transferred, the atoms become ions (Ca^{2+}, Cl^- and Cl^-) and the compound formed is calcium chloride ($CaCl_2$).

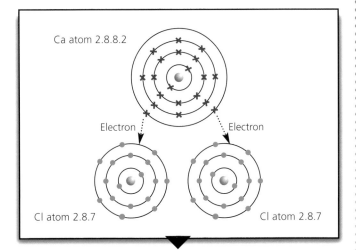

Ca atom 2.8.8.2

Electron · · · · Electron

Cl atom 2.8.7   Cl atom 2.8.7

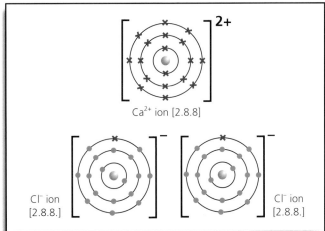

Ca^{2+} ion [2.8.8]

Cl^- ion [2.8.8.] Cl^- ion [2.8.8.]

Example 3 – Magnesium Oxide

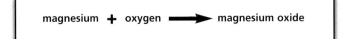

magnesium + oxygen ⟶ magnesium oxide

The magnesium atom (Mg) has 2 electrons in its outer shell. They are transferred to the oxygen atom (O). They now both have 8 electrons in their outer shells. The atoms have become ions (Mg^{2+} and O^{2-}) and the compound formed is magnesium oxide (MgO).

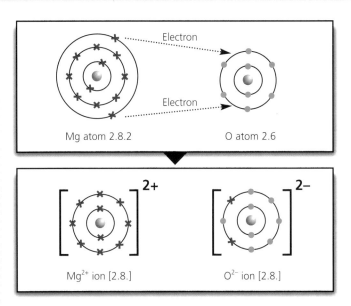

Electron

Electron

Mg atom 2.8.2   O atom 2.6

Mg^{2+} ion [2.8.] O^{2-} ion [2.8.]

Giant Ionic Structures

Compounds with ionic bonding are held together in a regular structure called a **giant lattice**.

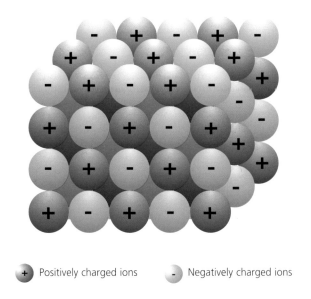

(+) Positively charged ions   (-) Negatively charged ions

Properties of Ionic Compounds

Compounds with ionic bonding…

- are crystalline solids
- have high melting and boiling points because the ions are held together by strong forces of attraction between oppositely charged ions
- are usually soluble in water and insoluble in organic solvents
- conduct electricity when they are melted or dissolved in water, as the ions are then free to move.

Forensic Science

Covalent Bonding

Covalent bonding occurs between **non-metal** atoms. It involves atoms **sharing** electrons in order to obtain the electronic structure of a Group 8 (0) element, i.e. a full outer shell of electrons.

Example – Chlorine Molecule

A chlorine molecule is made up of two chlorine atoms. An atom of chlorine (Cl) has 7 electrons so it needs 1 electron to fill its outer shell. So, two chlorine atoms combine, each sharing an electron to make a chlorine molecule. Both chlorine atoms now have 8 electrons in their outer energy shells.

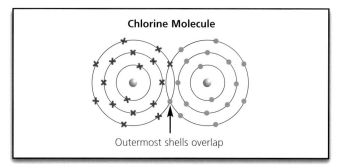

Chlorine Molecule

Outermost shells overlap

Carbon dioxide (CO_2) and water (H_2O) are two other examples of covalently bonded compounds:

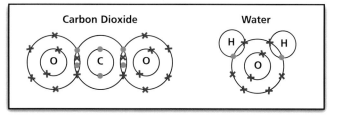

Carbon Dioxide　　　　**Water**

Organic Compounds

Many substances from living organisms are **organic compounds** with covalent bonding. They all contain the element **carbon**.

Examples of organic compounds include ethanol (C_2H_5OH) and glucose ($C_6H_{12}O_6$), and polymers like starch and glycogen, which are made up of glucose monomers.

Giant Covalent Structures

Graphite (a form of carbon) has a giant covalent structure or lattice. In this structure, each carbon atom forms three covalent bonds with other carbon

atoms. This builds a layered structure in which layers can slide past each other. There are weak forces of attraction between the layers, resulting in free electrons. This enables graphite to conduct electricity.

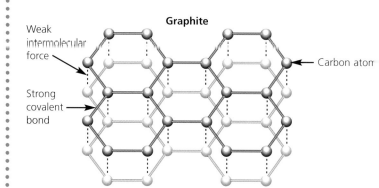

Graphite

Weak intermolecular force

Strong covalent bond

Carbon atom

Silicon dioxide has a giant covalent structure where each oxygen atom is joined to two silicon atoms and each silicon atom is joined to four oxygen atoms. The large number of covalent bonds results in silicon dioxide having a very high melting point.

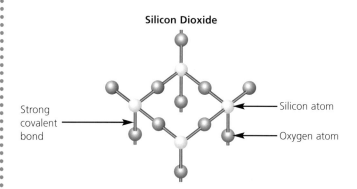

Silicon Dioxide

Strong covalent bond

Silicon atom

Oxygen atom

Properties of Covalent Compounds

Atoms which share electrons form molecules in which there are **strong covalent bonds** between the atoms in each molecule, but **weak intermolecular forces** (forces between molecules).

Compounds with covalent bonding…
- may be solids, liquids or gases
- have low melting and boiling points because the molecules are held together by weak forces of attraction
- are often insoluble in water and soluble in organic solvents
- do not usually conduct electricity as the molecules do not have an overall electrical charge.

Analysing Evidence – Chemical Tests

Any samples sent for chemical analysis are tested to identify which substances are present. Some **qualitative** tests which can be done on samples include…

- measuring pH (see below)
- finding solublility in water (see opposite)
- identifying metal ions using flame tests (see p.42)
- identifying whether it is a carbonate (see p.42)
- identifying ions in a solution using precipitation reactions (see p.43)
- identifying the presence of ethanol (see p.44)
- identifying the presence of glucose (see p.44 and p.9)
- separating mixtures of coloured substances (see p.45).

Measuring pH

To find the pH of a sample, you can use an indicator such as **universal indicator**, which comes in two forms:

- universal indicator paper, which is dipped into a test sample
- universal indicator liquid, a few drops of which are added to a test sample.

The colour of the sample can then be compared to a colour chart (like the one below) to find the pH.

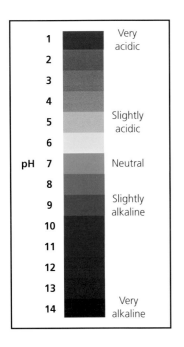

Solubility in Water

If a substance is soluble in water, it dissolves to form a clear solution. For example, salt dissolves in water to make salt solution.

The procedure to find out whether a sample is soluble in water is as follows:

1 Pour $5cm^3$ distilled water into a test tube. Use a spatula to add a small amount of the sample to the water. Shake the test tube thoroughly.

2 If it is hard to tell if the substance has dissolved, remove any undissolved material by filtration.

3 Place some of the filtrate on a watch glass and warm gently until all the water has evaporated. If you are left with a residue, this means that some of the substance has dissolved, which means it is soluble in water.

Obtaining a Clear Solution

You may need a clear solution if you wish to perform further tests on the sample. In order to obtain a clear solution, you should dissolve the sample in distilled water and then remove any undissolved material by filtering.

Forensic Science

Flame Tests

Flame tests can be used to identify some **metal ions** because they produce distinctive colours when heated in a flame.

The procedure is outlined below (see diagram opposite):

1 Dip a piece of nichrome (nickel–chromium alloy) wire in concentrated hydrochloric acid to clean it, then dip it in the sample.

2 Heat the wire in a Bunsen flame.

The following distinctive colours are produced:

- Yellow indicates sodium ions (Na^+) are present. Sodium ions are found in living cells, blood and urine.
- Lilac indicates potassium ions (K^+) are present. Potassium ions are found in all living cells.
- Brick red indicates calcium ions (Ca^{2+}) are present. Calcium ions are found in bones.
- Blue–green indicates copper ions (Cu^{2+}) are present. Copper ions are found in blood, the liver and hair.

Identifying Carbonates

Carbonates can be easily identified because they react ('fizz') with dilute acids to produce carbon dioxide gas (see diagram opposite).

The word equation for the reaction is…

For example, the equation for the reaction between calcium carbonate and dilute hydrochloric acid is…

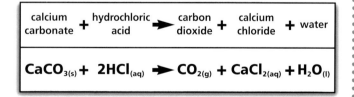

Test for Carbon Dioxide

When carbon dioxide is bubbled through **limewater**, a white solid precipitate appears, turning the clear limewater cloudy.

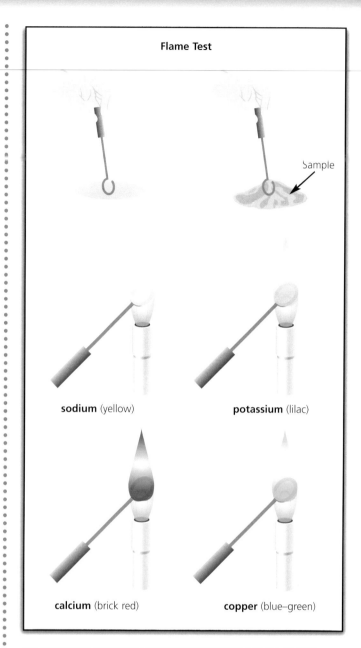

Flame Test

Sample

sodium (yellow)   **potassium** (lilac)

calcium (brick red)   **copper** (blue–green)

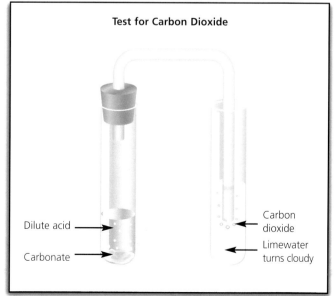

Test for Carbon Dioxide

Dilute acid

Carbonate

Carbon dioxide

Limewater turns cloudy

Identifying Ions by Precipitation Reactions

The ions present in a sample may be…

- **metal ions** (positive), e.g. calcium (Ca^{2+}), copper (Cu^{2+}), iron (Fe^{2+} and Fe^{3+}) and lead (Pb^{2+})
- **non-metal ions** (negative), e.g. chloride (Cl^-) and sulfate (SO_4^{2-}).

The ions can be identified when they form **precipitates**, i.e. insoluble salts that 'come out' of a solution.

Positive Ions

When sodium hydroxide solution (NaOH) is added to a solution of a sample, some metal ions present can be identified by the colour of the precipitate formed (see table 1 below).

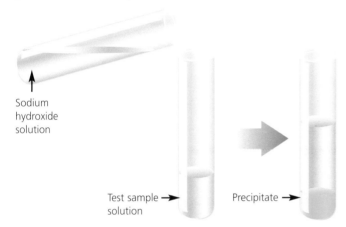

Sodium hydroxide solution

Test sample → solution

Precipitate →

Negative Ions

Non-metal ions present in a sample solution can be identified if they form precipitates with silver nitrate or barium chloride.

There are two tests that can be carried out:

- **Test 1**: Add a few drops of dilute nitric acid followed by a few drops of silver nitrate solution to a solution of the sample. If a white precipitate forms, it indicates that chloride ions (Cl^-) are present.
- **Test 2**: Add a few drops of dilute hydrochloric acid followed by a few drops of barium chloride solution to a solution of the sample. If a white precipitate forms, it indicates that sulfate ions (SO_4^{2-}) are present.

Example

Sodium hydroxide solution is added to a solution of an unknown substance. A green precipitate forms.

a) Which ions are present?

   Iron (II) ions

b) What precipitate is formed?

   Iron (II) hydroxide

c) Write a symbol equation for the reaction.

   $Fe^{2+}_{(aq)} + 2OH^-_{(aq)} \rightarrow Fe(OH)_{2(s)}$

1

Positive Ion	Test	Precipitate Formed	Symbol Equation
calcium, $Ca^{2+}_{(aq)}$	add sodium hydroxide	calcium hydroxide (white)	$Ca^{2+}_{(aq)} + 2OH^-_{(aq)} \rightarrow Ca(OH)_{2(s)}$
copper (II), $Cu^{2+}_{(aq)}$	add sodium hydroxide	copper (II) hydroxide (blue)	$Cu^{2+}_{(aq)} + 2OH^-_{(aq)} \rightarrow Cu(OH)_{2(s)}$
iron (II), $Fe^{2+}_{(aq)}$	add sodium hydroxide	iron (II) hydroxide (green)	$Fe^{2+}_{(aq)} + 2OH^-_{(aq)} \rightarrow Fe(OH)_{2(s)}$
iron (III), $Fe^{3+}_{(aq)}$	add sodium hydroxide	iron (III) hydroxide (brown)	$Fe^{3+}_{(aq)} + 3OH^-_{(aq)} \rightarrow Fe(OH)_{3(s)}$
lead, $Pb^{2+}_{(aq)}$	add sodium hydroxide	lead hydroxide (white), dissolves again when more sodium hydroxide solution is added	$Pb^{2+}_{(aq)} + 2OH^-_{(aq)} \rightarrow Pb(OH)_{2(s)}$

2

Negative Ion	Test	Precipitate Formed	Symbol Equation
chloride, Cl^-	add dilute nitric acid and silver nitrate solution	silver chloride (white)	$Ag^+_{(aq)} + Cl^-_{(aq)} \rightarrow AgCl_{(s)}$
sulfate, SO_4^{2-}	add dilute hydrochloric acid and barium chloride solution	barium sulfate (white)	$Ba^{2+}_{(aq)} + SO_4^{2+}_{(aq)} \rightarrow BaSO_{4(s)}$

Forensic Science

Test for Ethanol

To test if ethanol is present in a sample:

1 Add a few drops of dilute sulfuric acid to some potassium dichromate solution in a test tube.

2 Add a few drops of the test sample and gently warm the mixture.

If ethanol is present, orange potassium dichromate solution turns green.

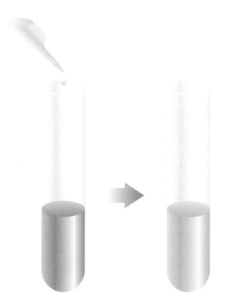

In this reaction, orange dichromate (VI) ions are reduced to green chromium (III) ions and ethanol is oxidised to ethanoic acid (vinegar). These reactions can be represented by the following equations:

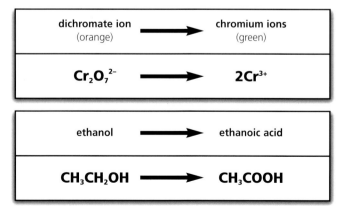

dichromate ion (orange)	→	chromium ions (green)
$Cr_2O_7^{2-}$	→	$2Cr^{3+}$

ethanol	→	ethanoic acid
CH_3CH_2OH	→	CH_3COOH

This is an example of a **redox** reaction: one reactant is **reduced** while the other reactant is **oxidised**.

Breathalysers are used to measure the concentration of ethanol in the breath of people suspected of driving under the influence of alcohol. The breathalyser contains sulfuric acid, orange potassium dichromate crystals and a catalyst (silver nitrate).

The driver is asked to breathe into the breathalyser through a tube. Any alcohol vapour in the breath turns the orange potassium dichromate crystals green. The degree of the colour change is directly related to the level of ethanol in the driver's breath.

At present, the legal limit of blood alcohol concentration (BAC) whilst driving a vehicle is 0.08g, or 80mg ethanol per 100cm³ blood. This corresponds to 35mg ethanol per 100cm³ breath.

If a person 'fails' the breathalyser test (i.e. the breathalyser registers more than 80mg ethanol per 100cm³) he or she will be asked to give a blood sample at the police station. The BAC can then be measured more accurately using a digital sensor machine.

Identifying Glucose

Benedict's test can be used to find out if glucose is present in a sample (see p.9).

Analysing Mixtures of Coloured Substances

Forensic scientists use chromatography to separate, compare and identify samples of ink, food colourings or lipstick. Paper or thin-layer chromatography (TLC) can be used. The solvent can be water or a non-aqueous solvent, e.g. propanone (acetone).

Chromatography separates substances according to differences in…

- **solubility** – how well a substance dissolves in a solvent; more soluble substances travel further.
- **adsorption** – how well a substance 'sticks' to the surface of the paper or thin layer; the more the substance sticks, the less easily it moves along the chromatogram.

Chromatography Procedure

To separate a mixture of coloured inks or dyes:

1. Draw a pencil line 1.5cm from the bottom of the paper or TLC plate. This is the **spot origin line**.
2. Use a capillary tube to put small drops of the unknown ink (X) and other samples which may contain the same ink (A, B, C, D and E) along the pencil line. Allow the spots to dry.
3. Pour the solvent into the tank to a depth of 1cm. Place the paper or TLC plate in the solvent and place the lid on the tank. Make sure the sample spots remain above the solvent so they are not washed off (see diagram A).
4. Remove the paper or TLC plate when the solvent has travelled near to the top of it, and allow it to dry.
5. Mark the centre of each coloured spot with a pencil. Measure the distance between this mark and the origin line. Also measure the distance between the origin line and the solvent front (see diagram B).
6. Calculate the retention factor, R_f, for each ink using the following formula:

$$R_f = \frac{\text{Distance moved by spot}}{\text{Distance moved by solvent}}$$

Example

Identify the unknown ink, X, in the chromatogram shown in the diagram below.

The unknown ink, X, is the same as Ink D because it contains the same dyes.

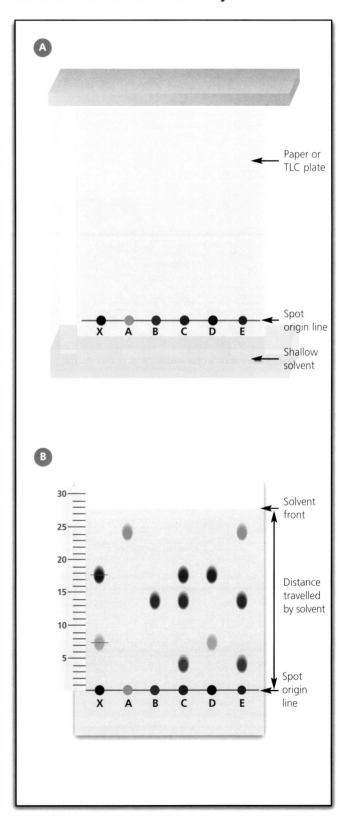

Forensic Science

Using Microscopes to Analyse Evidence

Forensic scientists need to examine evidence found at a crime scene, for example, soil, hair and fibre samples, and bullets. The evidence can be compared with samples found on a suspect's shoes or other belongings. If they are identical then it is likely that the suspect was present at the crime scene.

Microscopes can be used to analyse and compare distinctive features of different types of evidence (see p.47–48), to enable samples to be matched.

Light Microscope

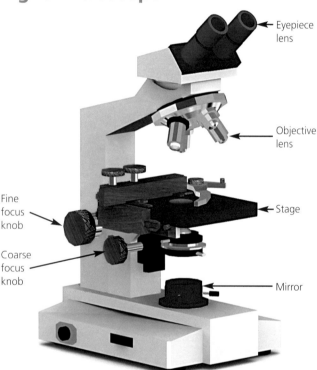

A **light microscope** has a mirror to **reflect** light up and through the object on the stage. The light rays are **focused** using convex glass lenses in the eyepiece and the objective lens which **refract** (bend) light rays. The focus knobs are used to move the lenses so that the object on the stage can be seen clearly.

A light microscope can magnify something up to about 400 times its original size. The detail that can be seen using a light microscope is limited because of the wavelength of light.

Light microscopes are used in school laboratories to magnify samples. Forensic scientists use more expensive and powerful equipment for more detailed analysis, often on minute quantities of material. The microscopes they use include...

- electron microscopes
- comparison microscopes
- polarising microscopes.

Electron Microscope

In an **electron microscope**, a beam of electrons is focused using electromagnets. The wavelength of electron beams is shorter than the wavelength of visible light, which is why an electron microscope has a higher **resolution** than a light microscope. (Resolution refers to how close two points in the image can be before they blur into one point and are no longer seen as two separate points.) The electron microscope can magnify an object up to 1 million times its original size.

Comparison Microscope

A **comparison microscope** links two microscopes together so two objects can be viewed at the same time. This allows the scientist to magnify items found at a crime scene and compare them with samples taken from a suspect, for example, fibres, seeds, bullets and paint.

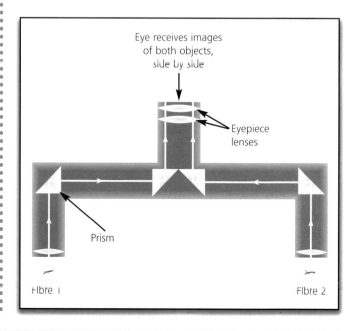

Polarising Microscope

White light is made up of light waves travelling in all directions. A **polarising microscope** has two polarising filters – the polariser and the analyser – which only allow light to pass through in one plane. A sample is placed on the microscope stage and rotated in the polarised light. As the sample rotates, the polarised light shining through the sample changes colour.

Minerals and **crystals** in soil samples or the **pigments** in layers of paint can be identified by the colours they produce when they rotate in polarised light.

Types of Evidence Analysed Using Microscopes

Soil

Soils from different places have different proportions of sand, clay and plant material, and different pHs. Soil can be analysed using a microscope to find…

- the colour
- the size of the particles it contains, e.g. large sand crystals or small clay particles
- if it contains any plant materials, e.g. pieces of dead plants, leaves, twigs or pollen.

Hair

A light microscope or comparison microscope can be used to look at hair samples to find out…

- whether it is from a human or an animal (most animal hairs have scales)
- which part of the body the hair came from
- the colour, and whether it is natural or dyed
- the shape, e.g. curly or straight
- the length
- whether it fell out naturally, was cut or was pulled out (by seeing if the follicle is intact).

Fibres

Fibres collected at a crime scene can come from a variety of origins. It is possible to identify fibres by studying them under a light microscope:

- **natural fibres** come from animals and plants
- **synthetic (manufactured) fibres**.

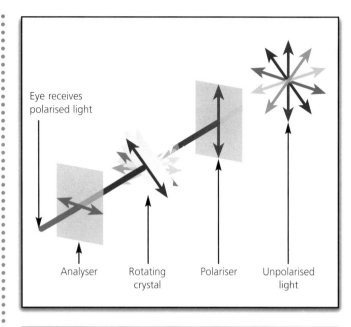

Eye receives polarised light

Analyser | Rotating crystal | Polariser | Unpolarised light

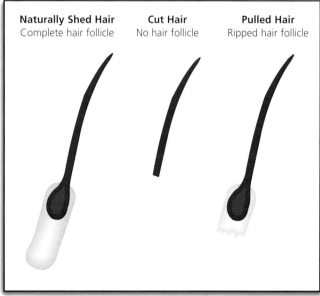

Naturally Shed Hair
Complete hair follicle

Cut Hair
No hair follicle

Pulled Hair
Ripped hair follicle

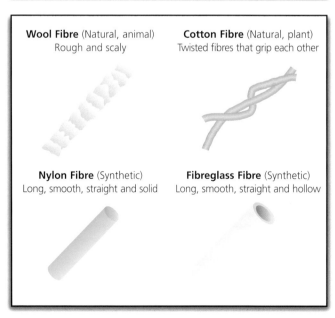

Wool Fibre (Natural, animal)
Rough and scaly

Cotton Fibre (Natural, plant)
Twisted fibres that grip each other

Nylon Fibre (Synthetic)
Long, smooth, straight and solid

Fibreglass Fibre (Synthetic)
Long, smooth, straight and hollow

Forensic Science

Seeds

Seeds may be found in soil samples. The seeds from different plants can be identified because they are different shapes, sizes and colours. Some examples are shown below:

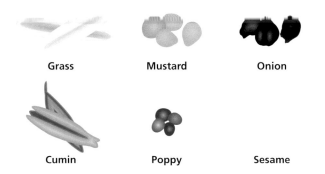

Grass	Mustard	Onion

Cumin	Poppy	Sesame

Pollen Grains

Pollen grains may also be found in soil samples. They are too small to be seen without using a microscope. An electron microscope may be needed to magnify the grains so that the shape can be seen clearly. The pollen produced by each species of plant has a recognisable shape and size. Two examples are shown below:

Hollyhock   Pine

Bullets

As a bullet passes down a gun barrel, microscopic scratches from the gun barrel mark the bullet's casing. These scratch marks, called **striations**, are rather like a fingerprint, because they are unique to the particular gun that fired the bullet.

For example, the police might find a weapon they suspect was used to fire a bullet found at a crime scene. A test bullet can be fired through the suspect weapon. A comparison microscope can then be used to compare the marks on this bullet with those on the bullet recovered from the crime scene. The bullets are rotated under the microscope to see if the marks match. If they match, it indicates that the weapon was used to fire the bullet found at the crime scene. If they do not match, it shows that the weapon was not used to fire the bullet found at the crime scene.

Example

Bullet A was found at a crime scene. Bullet B is a test bullet fired from a weapon suspected of being used at the crime scene. Is it likely that the suspect weapon was used to fire the bullet found at the crime scene?

The marks on the bullets are not identical, which means they were fired from different guns. So the suspected weapon was not used to fire the bullet that was found at the crime scene.

Paint Samples

A microscope can be used to examine the layer structure of a paint chip to find…

- the number of layers
- the order the layers were painted in
- the colour of each layer
- the texture of each layer
- the relative thickness of each layer.

Magnified Cross-section of a Paint Chip

Car body paint can consist of up to 14 layers of paint, e.g. primer, paint, lacquer, etc. The layers and colours of paint are unique to different manufacturers. This means that by examining a paint chip it may be possible to find the make, model, colour, previous colour(s) and year of manufacture of the car it came from.

Sometimes it is possible to fit together larger pieces of paint like a jigsaw puzzle.

Analysing Blood

Blood typing is used on a blood sample to find out…
- if it is from a human or an animal
- which blood group it belongs to (if it is human).

For the composition of blood see p.54.

Blood Groups

There are four main blood groups: **A**, **B**, **AB** and **O**. The groups are determined by the **antigens** (markers) present on the surface of the red blood cells.

There are two types of antigens, **A** and **B**:
- Blood group A has A antigens only.
- Blood group B has B antigens only.
- Blood group AB has both A and B antigens.
- Blood group O has neither A nor B antigens.

Plasma contains **antibodies**:
- People with blood group A have anti-B antibodies.
- People with blood group B have anti-A antibodies.
- People with blood group AB have neither anti-A nor anti-B antibodies.
- People with blood group O have both anti-A and anti-B antibodies.

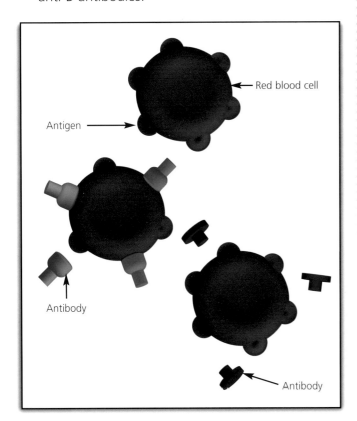

To find the blood group of a sample of blood, a blood grouping card is used. This has solutions of anti-A and anti-B antibodies on it. A sample of the blood to be analysed is mixed with anti-A antibodies. Another sample of the same blood is mixed with anti-B antibodies:
- If the red blood cells clump together when they are mixed with anti-A antibodies only, the blood is from a person with blood group A.
- If the red blood cells clump together when they are mixed with anti-B antibodies only, the blood is from a person with blood group B.
- If the red blood cells clump together when they are mixed with both anti-A and anti-B antibodies, the blood is from a person with blood group AB.
- If the red blood cells do not clump together when they are mixed with either anti-A or anti-B antibodies, the blood is from a person with blood group O.

Example

A blood sample is taken from a suspect. The blood is mixed with anti-A antibodies and anti-B antibodies. From the results below, what blood type is this person?

Anti-A	Anti-B	Control

Name.... **Suspect A** ....

Date.... **12.1.2007** ....

Test result................................. Group ☐

The blood clumped together when it was mixed with anti-B antibodies, but not when it was mixed with anti-A antibodies, so the person has blood group B.

Forensic Science

Analysing DNA

DNA (**d**eoxyribo**n**ucleic **a**cid) is found in the nucleus of each cell. DNA molecules are very long and form structures called **chromosomes**. The nucleus of most human cells contains 46 chromosomes. A section of chromosome is called a **gene**. Genes carry instructions that control the characteristics of an organism.

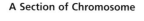

A Section of Chromosome

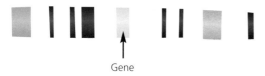

Gene

Each person inherits slightly different genes from their parents which is why everyone looks different. Unless you have an identical twin, your **genetic profile** (sometimes referred to as 'genetic fingerprint') is different from that of anyone else.

DNA Profiling

Forensic scientists can extract DNA from samples of blood, semen or saliva. They can then analyse the DNA from the samples using the following method:

1. The DNA is cut up into different sized fragments using **enzymes**.
2. The DNA fragments are separated in a gel medium placed in an electric field. This process is called **gel electrophoresis**.
3. The negatively charged DNA fragments move towards the positive electrode. The smaller DNA fragments move furthest.
4. A radioactive substance is used to label the DNA fragments, which are then X-rayed.

Forensic scientists can then compare the DNA profile from a suspect to samples of DNA found at a crime scene. If the DNA profiles match, then the suspect must have been present at the crime scene.

DNA profiling can also be used to show whether or not people are blood relatives.

Gel Electrophoresis

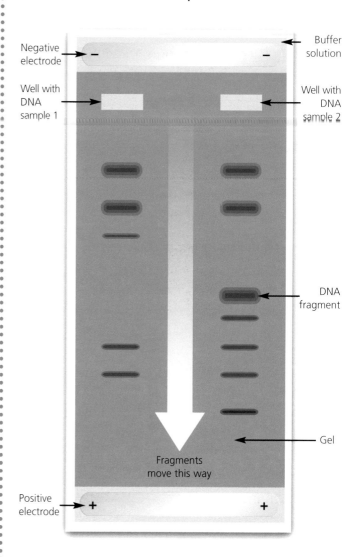

Negative electrode

Buffer solution

Well with DNA sample 1

Well with DNA sample 2

DNA fragment

Fragments move this way

Gel

Positive electrode

Example

The DNA profiles below show samples taken from a crime scene, two suspects and a victim. Can the DNA profile be used to prove that either of the suspects was present at the crime scene?

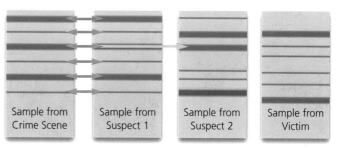

Sample from Crime Scene

Sample from Suspect 1

Sample from Suspect 2

Sample from Victim

The blood found at the crime scene matches the blood sample from Suspect 1, so that person must have been present at the crime scene.

Analysing Glass and Plastic

Forensic scientists can find the **refractive index, *n*,** of small fragments of glass or plastic from a crime scene and compare them to samples found on a suspect's clothing, or in a vehicle that may have been involved in a road traffic accident.

Refractive Index, *n*

Light changes direction when it crosses a boundary between two transparent materials of different **densities**. The refractive index is a measure of the amount that light bends or refracts when it passes through a substance.

Block of Glass or Plastic

To find the refractive index of a block of glass or plastic:

1. Place the block in the centre of a piece of paper and draw round it with a pencil.
2. Remove the block and use a protractor to draw the normal at 90° to the block.
3. Replace the block. Angle a ray box (with a single slit) so that the incident ray meets the corner formed by the normal and the boundary between the block and the air.
4. Mark the paths of the incident ray and the refracted ray with crosses.
5. Remove the block and draw in the paths of the rays. Join the points where the rays meet the boundaries between the block and the air to show the path of the light through the block.

6. Measure the angle of incidence, i, and the angle of refraction, r.
7. Use the refractive index formula below:

$$\text{Refractive index, } n = \frac{\text{Sine of angle of incidence (i)}}{\text{Sine of angle of refraction (r)}}$$

Small Fragment of Glass

Forensic scientists use a different method to find the refractive index of small fragments of glass. The fragment is placed in a drop of oil on the heated stage of a microscope:

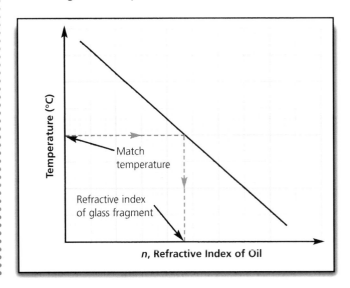

At first, the glass fragment can be seen. As the oil is heated up, there is a point at which the refractive index of the oil equals the refractive index of the glass fragment, and the fragment seems to disappear. The temperature at which the fragment can no longer be seen is called the **match temperature**.

At this temperature, the refractive index of the glass is the same as the refractive index of the oil it is immersed in. The refractive index of the glass can be found from a graph of the refractive index of the oil against temperature.

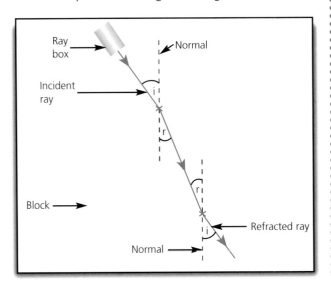

Forensic Science

Types of Fingerprints

Fingerprints can be sorted into three groups:

Arch	Loop	Whorl

Some fingerprints may have several of the patterns joined together. No two people, not even identical twins, have the same pattern of arches, loops and whorls. This means it is possible to identify a suspect from his / her fingerprints.

When the police question suspects they also take their fingerprints. The fingerprints can then be compared to those found at the crime scene. If there is a match at 16 or more points between a suspect's fingerprint and that found at the crime scene, the fingerprint can be used as evidence in court (see diagram below).

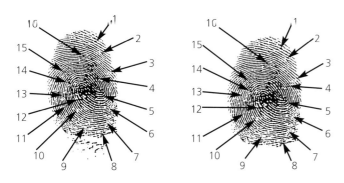

Fingerprints from the crime scene can also be compared with those held in a police database. If there is no match, it means the suspect has not been convicted of a crime before.

Using Databases

The police use different databases to provide them with information to assist in their enquiries. You need to be able to…
- explain how to record a witness statement
- describe the type of information stored in databases used by forensic scientists
- explain how databases can be searched.

Records used to be kept mainly on paper. However, the majority are now kept on computer.

A **database** is a collection of millions of files of information or data stored in a computer.

Some examples of databases are listed below:
- **Fingerprint database** on the Police National Computer (PNC).
- **DVLA** (Driver and Vehicle Licensing Agency) database which includes the number plate, make, model and colour of a vehicle, together with the name and address of the current owner, and whether or not the road tax has been paid up to date.
- **DNA databases** have DNA profiles and are used to identify someone from a hair, blood, semen or saliva sample.
- **Police records** include descriptions of missing persons.
- **Medical records** have details of patients' vaccinations, operations, and X-rays showing broken bones.
- **Insurance company records** have details of valuable items which can be used to identify the owners of stolen items that have been recovered.
- **Gun and bullet type records** help to trace the make and model of a gun from a bullet found at a crime scene.
- **Dental records** include details of fillings and missing teeth and may help to identify a body (see example on p.53).

In a database, data is arranged so it can be…
- viewed
- sorted to look for patterns
- edited to keep it up to date
- searched in different ways to find the answers to different questions.

Some advantages of a computer database compared to paper records:
- new data can be added easily
- data can be easily updated or amended, for example, changing a person's address when he / she moves house
- large amounts of data (millions of records) can be easily sorted or searched in a short period of time
- many people within an organisation can gain access to the information at the same time, regardless of their location.

DENTAL RECORD

LAST NAME		FIRST NAME		SEX
				M / F

ESTIMATED AGE	ETHNIC ORIGIN

DATE OF RECONSTRUCTION	
	I.D. NUMBER

RIGHT
1 2 3 4 5 6 7 8 9 10 11 12 13 14 15 16
32 31 30 29 28 27 26 25 24 23 22 21 20 19 18 17
LEFT

1.	
2.	
3.	
4.	
5.	
6.	
7.	
8.	
9.	
10.	
11.	
12.	
13.	
14.	
15.	
16.	
17.	
18.	
19.	
20.	
21.	
22.	
23.	
24.	
25.	
26.	
27.	
28.	
29.	
30.	

CAPMI SYMBOLS

PRIMARY CODES		SECONDARY CODES	
C	CROWN	A	ANOMALY, ROOT TIP, ANY PATHOLOGY
D	DISTAL		
F	FACIAL	B	PRIMARY TOOTH
L	LINGUAL	G	GOLD, CAST METAL, STAINLESS STEEL
M	MESIAL		
O	OCCLUSAL/INCISAL	N	NON-METALLIC RESTORATION
U	UNERUPTED		
V	VIRGIN TOOTH	P	PONTIC
X	MISSING TOOTH	R	ROOT CANAL FILLING
/	JAW FRAGMENT MISSING, NONRECOGNIZABLE FRACTURED CROWN, TRAUMATIC AVULSION	S	SILVER AMALGAM
		T	REMOVABLE PROS
		Z	CARIES

Interpreting and Presenting Evidence

Forensic scientists have to prepare a report of their findings. You need to be able to…
- draw conclusions based on evidence
- use evidence to determine whether a suspect may have been present at a crime scene.

Once a forensic scientist has analysed the evidence he / she has to write a report. The report will contain details of the findings and the conclusions that have been drawn based on the investigations that were carried out.

When writing a report, a forensic scientist needs to make sure that…
- everything that is contained in the report is based on evidence
- the evidence is presented clearly and logically
- the conclusions drawn from the evidence are explained.

Remember, the report that a forensic scientist produces may be presented in court, therefore it needs to be accurate and reliable. Unreliable or inaccurate evidence could lead to a miscarriage of justice, i.e. an innocent person being convicted of a crime. It could also lead to cases being dismissed, or guilty people not being convicted.

In this revision guide, drawing conclusions from evidence has been covered alongside analysing evidence (see p.47–52).

Sports Science

Exercise and the Human Body

Understanding the body's functions can help sports physiologists develop personal training programmes to enable athletes to improve their performance. You need to be able to…

- describe the structure and function of the cardiovascular system
- describe aerobic and anaerobic respiration
- describe the effect of exercise on the human body
- explain how and why the body maintains constant internal conditions
- describe how muscles work
- measure physiological changes such as pulse rate, breathing rate and tidal volume
- explain the importance of taking accurate and reliable measurements.

Performance in Sport

Success in sport depends on many factors, including the athlete's…

- fitness
- skill level
- ability to concentrate and focus in a competitive situation
- intake of energy and nutrients before exercise
- sports equipment and clothing.

There are different types of **sports scientists** who help athletes to improve their performance in different ways.

Sports physiologists have a detailed understanding of the organ systems of the body. They can help an athlete develop a personal fitness programme designed to meet his / her individual needs.

Nutritionists and **dieticians** can advise an athlete on the best foods to eat in order to optimise his / her performance.

Materials scientists develop the materials that are used in sports equipment and clothing.

Blood

If blood is allowed to stand without clotting, it separates out into four components:

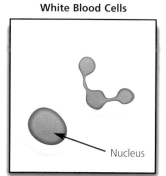

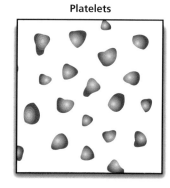

Plasma is a straw-coloured liquid which transports…

- carbon dioxide from the organs to the lungs
- glucose from the small intestine to the organs
- waste products (e.g. urea) from the liver to the kidneys.

White blood cells have a nucleus which is variable in shape. Some types of white cells engulf invading microorganisms in order to defend the body. Others produce antibodies to attack microorganisms.

Red blood cells transport oxygen from the lungs to the organs. They have no nucleus so they can contain lots of haemoglobin (the red pigment which carries oxygen). In the lungs, haemoglobin combines with oxygen to form oxyhaemoglobin. When oxyhaemoglobin reaches other tissues, it splits up into haemoglobin and oxygen.

Platelets are tiny pieces of red blood cells which have no nucleus. They clump together when a blood vessel is damaged and form a mesh of fibres in order to produce a clot.

Organs and Systems

Each **organ** in the body has a specific job. For example, the heart pumps blood around the body, and the lungs exchange gases.

Organs are made of **tissues**. A tissue is a group of similar cells that work together. The heart is made of muscle tissue, nervous tissue and connective tissue.

Organs cannot work by themselves; they depend on other organs to supply the substances they need. So, organs are linked together to form **organ systems**, for example…

- the **cardiovascular** (circulatory) **system** transports substances around the body
- the **gas exchange** (breathing) **system** takes in oxygen and removes carbon dioxide
- the **excretory system** removes waste products, e.g. urea, and maintains the balance of water in the body
- the **musculo-skeletal system** provides support and protection for the body, and places for muscles to attach.

The Cardiovascular System

The human cardiovascular system consists of the heart, blood vessels and blood. The system carries blood from the heart to all the cells of the body to provide them with glucose and oxygen. It also carries waste products, including carbon dioxide, away from the cells. Blood is pumped to the lungs so that the carbon dioxide can be exchanged for oxygen.

The heart acts as a pump in a **double circulatory system**. Blood flows around a 'figure of eight' circuit and passes through the heart twice on each circuit. Blood travels away from the heart through the **arteries** and returns to the heart through the **veins**.

There are two separate circulation systems:
- One loop carries blood from the heart to the lungs, and then back to the heart.
- The other loop carries blood from the heart to all other parts of the body, and then back to the heart.

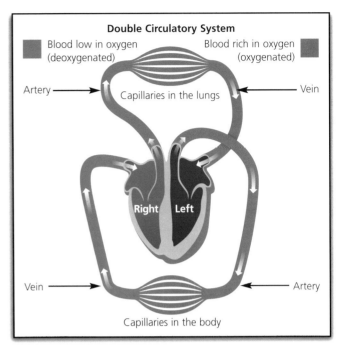

Double Circulatory System

Blood low in oxygen (deoxygenated)　　Blood rich in oxygen (oxygenated)

Artery　　Capillaries in the lungs　　Vein

Right　Left

Vein　　Artery

Capillaries in the body

The Heart

The **heart** is a muscular pump; most of the wall of the heart is made of **muscle**.

Atria are the smaller, less muscular upper chambers, which receive blood coming back to the heart through the veins.

Ventricles are the larger, more muscular lower chambers, which pump blood out of the heart. The left ventricle is more muscular than the right since it has to pump blood around the whole body.

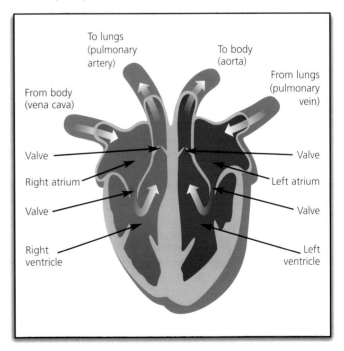

To lungs (pulmonary artery)　　To body (aorta)

From body (vena cava)　　From lungs (pulmonary vein)

Valve　　Valve

Right atrium　　Left atrium

Valve　　Valve

Right ventricle　　Left ventricle

Sports Science

The Heart (cont.)

How the Heart Pumps Blood

When the heart muscle relaxes, blood from the lungs and the rest of the body flows through veins into the atria. The atria then contract, squeezing blood into the ventricles.

When the ventricles contract, blood is forced out of them into the arteries, which carry blood to the body and the lungs. The heart muscle then relaxes and the whole process starts again.

Blood Vessels

There are three types of blood vessel: arteries, veins and capillaries.

Arteries carry blood away from the heart. They have thick elastic walls to cope with the high pressure of blood expelled from the heart. The blood they carry is rich in oxygen and glucose.

Veins carry blood towards the heart. They have thinner, less elastic walls, and contain valves to prevent blood flowing backwards. The blood they carry is rich in carbon dioxide and waste, e.g. urea.

Valves make sure that the blood flows in the right direction, i.e. not backwards.

Capillaries connect arteries to veins. They have a narrow, thin wall which is only one cell thick. The exchange of substances between cells and blood takes place here.

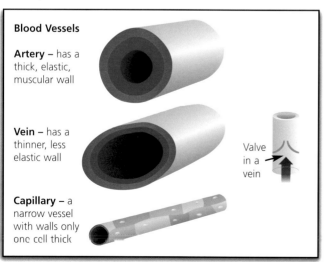

Blood Vessels

Artery – has a thick, elastic, muscular wall

Vein – has a thinner, less elastic wall

Valve in a vein

Capillary – a narrow vessel with walls only one cell thick

Exchange of Substances at the Capillaries

Exchange of substances between the blood and cells in organs such as the heart, lungs and muscles takes place in the capillaries, for example:

- glucose in plasma diffuses from the blood into the cells
- oxygen (carried as oxyhaemoglobin in red blood cells) diffuses from the blood into the cells
- carbon dioxide diffuses out of the cells into the plasma
- urea and other waste substances diffuse out of the cells into the plasma.

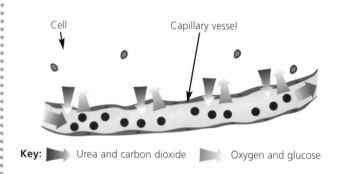

Cell   Capillary vessel

Key: ▶ Urea and carbon dioxide   ▶ Oxygen and glucose

Heart / Pulse Rate

Heart rate (pulse rate) is the number of times a person's heart 'beats' per minute, i.e. the number of times the ventricles contract each minute.

Arterial pulse is a pressure wave that travels along the thick elastic wall of an artery. It corresponds with the contraction of the ventricles.

The **pulse rate** is taken by pressing the index and middle fingers firmly but gently on an artery in the wrist or the neck, and counting how many beats there are in a minute.

The **resting heart rate** is the number of times the heart beats each minute when a person is completely relaxed, rested and not moving. An average resting heart rate is between 60 and 80 beats per minute. To make sure that the measurements are **valid**, the pulse rate should be measured three times and an average found.

The Gas Exchange System

The thorax (chest cavity, see diagram A) contains...

- the trachea – a flexible tube surrounded by rings of cartilage, which prevent it from collapsing
- bronchi – branches of the trachea
- bronchioles – branches of a bronchus
- alveoli – millions of tiny air sacs where gas exchange takes place
- the diaphragm – a muscular 'sheet' between the thorax and abdomen
- ribs – to protect the contents of the thorax
- rib muscles – to raise and lower the ribs.

Gas Exchange in the Alveoli

The **alveoli** (see diagram B) have a large, moist surface area and an excellent capillary blood supply, so they make the lungs very efficient at exchanging carbon dioxide and oxygen.

The alveoli are very close to blood capillaries so carbon dioxide can diffuse from the plasma into the alveoli, and oxygen can diffuse from alveoli into the blood (see diagram C).

Ventilation

The gas exchange system is designed to allow oxygen and carbon dioxide to be efficiently exchanged. For this to happen, the lungs have to be constantly 'refreshed' by air.

To **inhale**, the rib muscles contract, pulling the ribcage upwards and outwards. The diaphragm contracts, causing it to flatten. These movements cause an increase in the volume of the thorax and, therefore, a decrease in air pressure, drawing atmospheric air into the lungs (see diagram D).

To **exhale**, the rib muscles relax, allowing the ribcage to move downwards. The diaphragm also relaxes. These movements cause a decrease in the volume of the thorax and, therefore, an increase in air pressure. This results in air being forced out of the lungs (see diagram E).

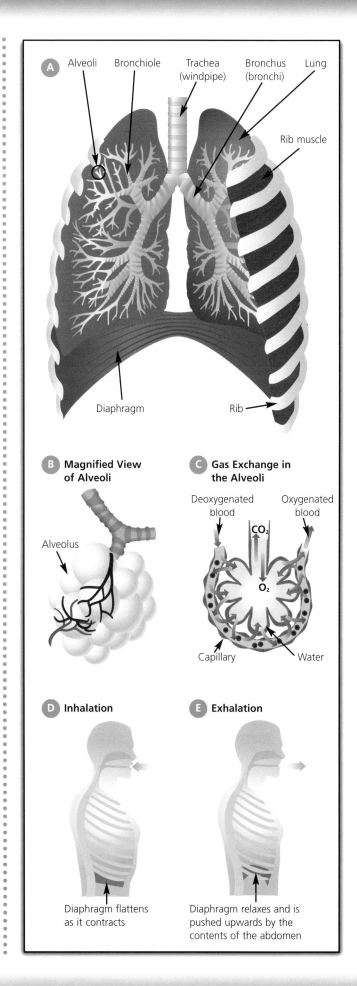

A — Alveoli, Bronchiole, Trachea (windpipe), Bronchus (bronchi), Lung, Rib muscle, Diaphragm, Rib

B Magnified View of Alveoli — Alveolus

C Gas Exchange in the Alveoli — Deoxygenated blood, Oxygenated blood, CO_2, O_2, Capillary, Water

D Inhalation — Diaphragm flattens as it contracts

E Exhalation — Diaphragm relaxes and is pushed upwards by the contents of the abdomen

Sports Science

Vital Capacity and Tidal Volume

Vital capacity is the maximum amount of air that you can breathe out after taking as deep a breath in as possible. It is found by breathing into a **spirometer**. The units of vital capacity are **dm³** (decimetres cubed).

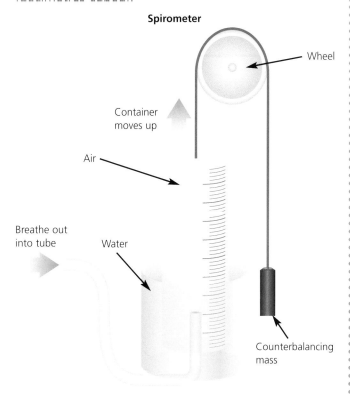

Spirometer

Tidal volume

Tidal volume is the volume of air that you breathe in and out when you are resting. It can be found using a spirometer. The spirometer prints out a pattern of your breathing.

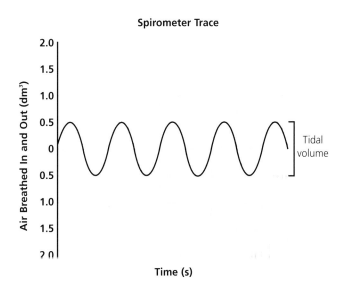

Spirometer Trace

Measuring Breathing Rate

Breathing rate is found by counting the number of breaths a person takes in one minute.

To make sure that the measurements are **valid**, the breathing rate should be counted three times and an average found.

Energy for Physical Activity

The cardiovascular system transports…
- oxygen from the lungs to the cells of the body
- glucose from the digestive system to the cells of the body.

In the cells, energy stored in glucose molecules is released during respiration.

Respiration may be **aerobic** or **anaerobic**.

Aerobic Respiration

Aerobic respiration is the release of energy from glucose by combining it with oxygen.

Aerobic respiration takes place in all living cells:

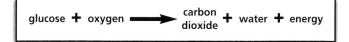

Aerobic respiration is a very efficient method of producing energy. It occurs during normal day-to-day activity and accounts for our energy production up to about 60% of maximum effort.

The drawback is that it cannot produce energy as quickly as anaerobic respiration (see p.59).

During aerobic respiration…
- glucose and oxygen are brought to the respiring cells by the bloodstream
- carbon dioxide is taken by the blood to the lungs, and breathed out
- water passes into the blood and is lost as sweat, moist breath and urine
- energy is used for muscle contraction, metabolism and maintaining a constant temperature.

Anaerobic Respiration

Anaerobic respiration is the fast release of a small amount of energy from glucose, in the absence of oxygen:

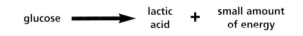

glucose ⟶ lactic acid **+** small amount of energy

Anaerobic respiration happens when the muscles need to work so hard that the lungs, heart and bloodstream cannot deliver enough oxygen for aerobic respiration.

Because the glucose is only partly broken down to lactic acid, only a small amount of energy is released.

Build up of lactic acid in the muscles results in acute fatigue in muscles and produces an **oxygen debt**. This 'debt' must be repaid by continued deep breathing after vigorous exercise in order to take in enough oxygen to oxidise the lactic acid into carbon dioxide and water.

Anaerobic respiration is an inefficient process since it produces only a twentieth of the energy that is produced during aerobic respiration (see p.58). However, it produces energy much faster and so is used during high intensity (explosive) activity over a short period. After a short time, the build up of lactic acid affects the performance of the muscles, making them feel tired and rubbery.

Effects of Exercise

When you exercise, your muscles need more **energy**. To release more energy, muscle cells need more glucose and oxygen for respiration so the...
- heart rate increases in order to pump blood around the body faster
- breathing rate increases in order to supply the blood with more oxygen and remove more carbon dioxide
- tidal volume increases so more air can be taken into the lungs with each breath.

As a result, the skin temperature rises, sweating increases, and muscles ache.

Before a sports physiologist can advise an athlete on an appropriate fitness programme, measurements of the athlete's heart rate and breathing rate before, during and after exercise need to be taken. The athlete's recovery rate can then be found.

Recovery rate is the time it takes for your heart rate and breathing rate to return to the normal resting rate after exercise.

Example
A boy's heart rate was measured before, during and after a 5-minute run until his heart rate returned to its resting rate. After a month's training his heart rate was measured before, during and after a 5-minute run.

The graph below shows the measurements before starting the training programme and after.

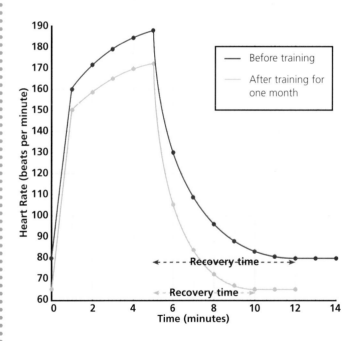

a) What is the boy's recovery rate...
   i) before training?
      7 minutes
   ii) after training for one month?
      5 minutes
b) What other differences in the boy's heart rate can you see from the graph?
   After training for a month, his resting heart rate was lower, and his heart rate did not increase as much during exercise.

Sports Science

Keeping Things Constant

There are many chemical reactions taking place inside the body. The reactions are controlled by enzymes which need certain conditions in order to work. Keeping conditions constant inside the body is called **homeostasis**.

The internal conditions that have to be controlled are temperature, water content, blood glucose, pH and carbon dioxide levels.

Temperature

Temperature is controlled by the **nervous system**. The core temperature of the body is kept at around 37°C because this is the ideal temperature for enzymes that are present in the human body.

Monitoring and control of temperature is carried out by the **thermoregulatory centre** in the brain. The brain has **receptors** that are sensitive to the temperature of the blood flowing through it. There are also temperature receptors in the skin which provide information about skin temperature.

When the body is too warm, blood vessels in the skin **dilate** (become wider). This causes more heat to be lost by radiation (making the skin look red). Sweat from sweat glands evaporates and cools the skin.

When the body is cold, blood vessels in the skin **constrict** (become narrower) in order to reduce heat loss by radiation. Muscles start to 'shiver' causing heat energy to be released from respiration in muscle cells.

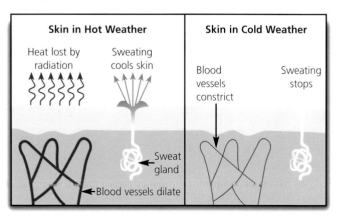

Water

Water makes up about 70% of the body's weight (see p.14). The body needs to maintain a constant amount of water in the cells to enable chemical reactions to take place.

Water is taken into the body by drinking fluids and eating food. Water is lost from the body by urinating, sweating and breathing.

The kidneys adjust the amount of urine to maintain the water balance:
- Drinking a lot of fluids causes the body to produce more urine because the blood becomes diluted, so the kidneys remove more water from it.
- Drinking very little fluid makes the blood more concentrated, so the kidneys remove less water and less urine is produced. (Less urine is also produced in hot conditions because more sweat is produced.)

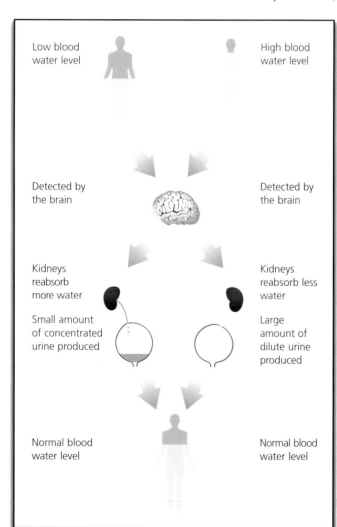

Glucose

Blood glucose concentration is monitored and controlled by the **pancreas**.

The pancreas secretes two **hormones**:
- **insulin**, which causes the liver to change glucose in the blood to insoluble glycogen
- **glucagon**, which causes the liver to change insoluble glycogen into glucose.

The pancreas adjusts the amount of insulin and glucagon released in order to keep the body's blood glucose levels as close to normal as possible:
- Eating a meal which is high in carbohydrates causes the blood glucose concentration to go up, so the pancreas produces insulin.
- Exercising causes the blood glucose concentration to go down, so the pancreas produces glucagon.

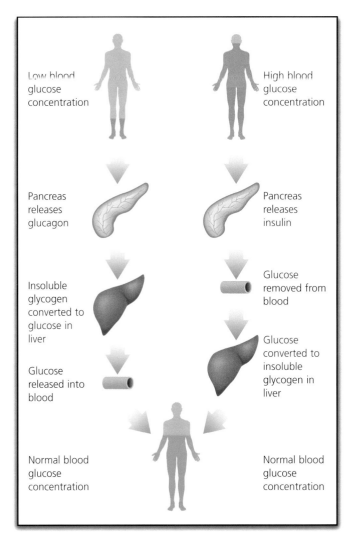

Measuring Glucose in the Body

Glucose content can be measured by testing the urine or the blood.

Testing Urine
1. Collect a urine sample.
2. Dip a test strip into the urine for 1–2 seconds.
3. Wait for 30 seconds, then compare the test strip with the colour chart.

The results are either negative or varying degrees of positive, indicating the different amounts of glucose that are present.

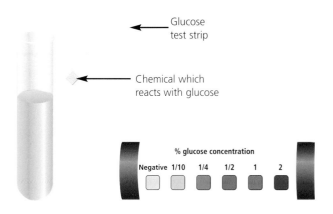

Testing Blood
1. Prick your finger with a sterile needle to produce a drop of blood.
2. Place the drop of blood on a test strip.
3. Put the strip into the blood glucose meter and read the blood glucose level.

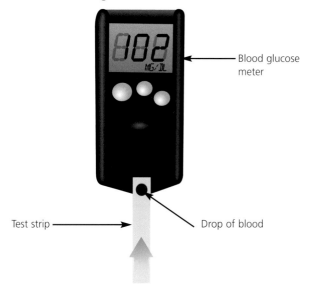

Sports Science

Muscles

Every movement of the body depends on **muscles**. Muscle tissue is made up of many muscle fibres (see diagram A).

Muscles are attached to the skeleton, usually across a joint, by **tendons**, which are fibrous and inelastic.

Muscles can only create movement by **contracting**. When a muscle contracts it gets shorter and pulls a bone. Because muscles can only contract, they always work in **antagonistic pairs**.

In an antagonistic pair, when one muscle **contracts**, the other muscle of the pair **relaxes**. For example…
- to bend the arm, the biceps contracts and the triceps relaxes (see diagram B)
- to straighten the arm, the biceps relaxes and the triceps contracts (see diagram C).

Measuring the Strength of a Muscle

The strength of a muscle can be measured by using a **grip test**. The scales or hand dynamometer should be gripped and squeezed as hard as possible (see diagram D). The strength is measured by the **force** exerted. Force is measured in **newtons (N)**.

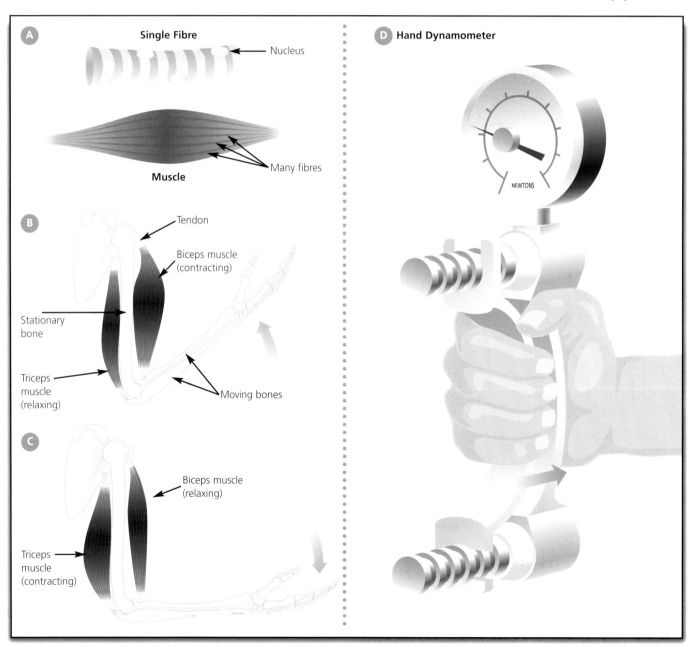

A

Single Fibre

Nucleus

Many fibres

Muscle

B

Tendon

Biceps muscle (contracting)

Stationary bone

Triceps muscle (relaxing)

Moving bones

C

Biceps muscle (relaxing)

Triceps muscle (contracting)

D Hand Dynamometer

NEWTONS

Sports Nutrition

Sports nutritionists and dieticians study athletes' nutrient intakes to provide advice to enable them to maximise their performance. You need to be able to…

- describe the factors that affect daily energy requirements
- calculate basic energy requirements (BER) and Body Mass Index (BMI)
- explain why different athletes have different diets
- compare and contrast different diets
- describe the composition of isotonic sports drinks.

Sports Nutrition

In order for athletes to optimise their performance, they must ensure that their diet contains the right balance of nutrients for their sport.

Sports nutritionists and dieticians study athletes' nutrient intakes, to enable them to be able to give advice to the athletes to help them maximise their performance during exercise.

Daily Energy Requirements

The amount of energy a person needs in a day depends on…

- his / her body size or mass
- how active he / she is
- how fast he / she is growing.

The energy a person uses when resting is called the **basal metabolic rate** (**BMR**) or **basic energy requirement** (**BER**). It varies according to a person's mass. BMR or BER is about 5.5 kilojoules per hour, or 1.3 kilocalories per hour, for every kilogram of body mass.

Energy Requirements

The food consumed in a day should provide a person with enough energy to get through that day. Even sleeping requires energy to keep…

- the heart beating
- the lungs working
- the body temperature constant
- all the chemical reactions in the body going.

Different amounts of energy are needed when you move around or exercise. The graph below shows approximate values for some activities.

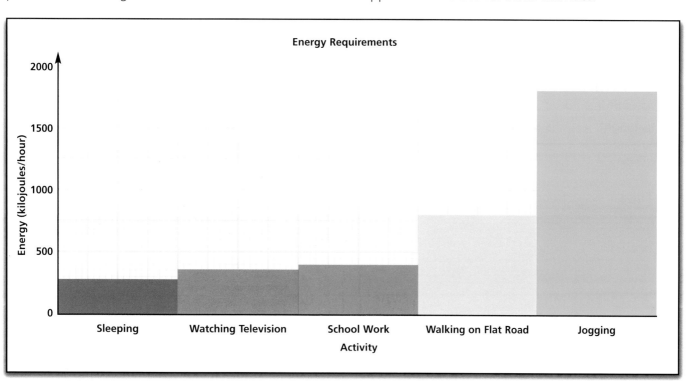

Energy Requirements (cont.)

You can calculate your actual daily energy and nutrient intake by keeping a **diet diary**. Record everything you eat and drink for at least three days and then find your **average daily intake** (see foot of page for an example of part of a diet diary).

Body Mass Index (BMI)

Body Mass Index (BMI) is an indicator of a person's ideal weight. It can be found using this formula:

$$\text{Body Mass Index} = \frac{\text{Body mass (kg)}}{\text{Height}^2\text{ (m}^2)}$$

BMI	What it Means
Under 20	Underweight (below ideal weight)
20–25	Ideal (ideal weight)
26–30	Overweight (above ideal weight)
Over 30	Obese (much too heavy; health risks)

Example

Calculate a man's BMI if he is 1.85m tall and has a mass of 74kg. What does the man's BMI tell you?

Use the formula…

$$\text{BMI} = \frac{\text{Body mass (kg)}}{\text{Height}^2\text{ (m}^2)}$$

$$= \frac{74}{1.85^2} = \textbf{22}$$

The ideal BMI is 20–25, so he is an ideal weight for his height.

Balanced Diet

The food and drink we consume each day makes up our diet.

A **balanced diet** provides you with the right amount of nutrients and energy to maintain a constant body mass. The intake of energy must match the body's needs – no more and no less.

The pie chart below shows the recommended ratio of carbohydrate, protein and fat for a balanced diet:

- 55–60% carbohydrate
- 25–30% fat
- 15–20% protein.

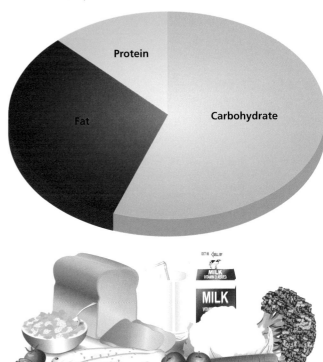

Diet Diary

Time	Food	How Much (g)	Energy (kJ)	Carbohydrate (kJ)	Protein (g)	Fat (g)
6.55 (breakfast)	cereal	45	900	37	9	3
	milk	70	180	3	2	2
	toast	35	320	17	3	0
	butter	5	160	0	0	5

Special Diets

Athletes follow the general guidelines for a balanced diet, but some alter the ratio of carbohydrate, protein and fat in their diet, depending upon the sports they participate in.

Strength Events

Athletes who rely upon strength for their sport (e.g. weightlifters, gymnastic rings athletes) often do a lot of weight training. Athletes who compete in this type of sport eat more protein (see p.9) to help their muscles grow and repair. The proteins are broken down into amino acids during digestion and are then restructured to form muscle protein.

Endurance Events

Athletes who compete in events which require a high level of endurance (e.g. marathon runners) often increase their complex carbohydrate (see p.8) intake just before a sporting event. The carbohydrates are broken down into glucose during digestion and are then recombined to form glycogen, which is stored in muscles and in the liver. During an athletic event, glycogen is broken down in respiration to release energy.

Isotonic Sports Drinks

During exercise, glycogen stores decrease as they are used to provide the body with energy. This is particularly noticeable during prolonged exercise.

The body also sweats during exercise in order to keep its core temperature at 37°C. Sweat contains water, and **ions** such as Cl^-, Ca^{2+}, Mg^{2+}, Na^+ and K^+. If the water and ions are not replaced, the body will become **dehydrated**.

Dehydration and depletion of the body's glycogen stores are two factors that can reduce an athlete's performance.

Isotonic sports drinks have been developed to help athletes perform better. Isotonic drinks have a similar ion (electrolyte) concentration to blood and other body fluids.

Isotonic sports drinks provide…
- water
- ions (electrolytes)
- simple carbohydrates, for example, glucose, in a concentration of between 6% and 8%.

Sports Science

Materials for Sport

Materials scientists develop and test new materials to help improve the performance of clothing and equipment for sports. You need to...

- know the structures, properties and examples of metals, polymers, ceramics and composites
- explain why certain properties are desirable in a material
- give the advantages and disadvantages of synthetic and natural materials
- explain why friction is important in the design of sports equipment and clothing
- be able to select suitable materials for sports clothing and equipment, and explain your choices.

Materials for Sport

Materials scientists research, develop and test new materials that could be used for equipment and clothing to help athletes improve their performance.

Types of Materials

Materials are sorted into groups that have similar structures and properties:

- polymers
- metals
- ceramics
- composites.

Polymers

Polymers are covalent compounds made up of chains of thousands of smaller units, called **monomers**, joined together.

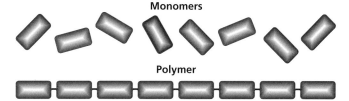

Polymers can be **natural**, for example, wool, cotton or silk, or **synthetic**, for example, nylon, lycra and melamine. Polymers may have a **linear** or **cross-linked** structure.

Structure of Linear Polymers

Linear polymers have long chains held in place by weak intermolecular forces.

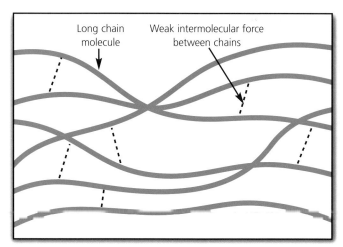

Some linear polymers also have coiled or zig-zag fibres. These are called **elastomers** (elastic polymers). The long, folded chains can be stretched, but will return to their original shape when the force is removed.

Unstretched – original shape

Stretched

Unstretched – returns to original shape

Examples and Uses – Natural Polymers

- **Cotton** – carbohydrate made up of sugar molecules joined together; used for clothing.
- **Rubber** (elastomer) – made from the sap (latex) of rubber trees; used for sports equipment like tennis balls.
- **Wool** and **silk** – proteins made up of amino acid molecules joined together; used for clothing.

Examples and Uses – Synthetic Polymers

- **Kevlar** (a 'super fibre', about five times stronger than steel) is used in bullet-proof vests, for strengthening boat rigging, and in the frames of tennis racquets.
- **Polyamide** (nylon) is used for clothing.
- **Polychloroethene** (PVC) is used for waterproof clothing and shoes.
- **Polyester** (PET) is used for clothing, and drinks bottles.
- **Polystyrene** is used for cycle helmets and protective clothing.
- **Polyurethane**, or lycra, (an elastomer) is used for sports clothing.
- **Silicone rubber** (an elastomer) is used for the soles of shoes, bicycle tyres, and balls, e.g. squash balls.

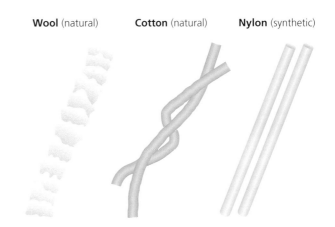

Wool (natural)   **Cotton** (natural)   **Nylon** (synthetic)

Structure of Cross-Linked Polymers

Cross-linked polymers have strong covalent bonds between adjacent chains.

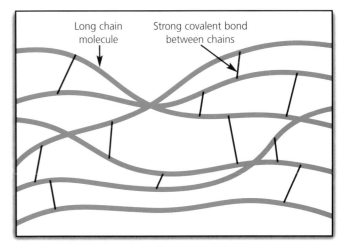

Long chain molecule   Strong covalent bond between chains

Examples and Uses

- **Epoxy resin** is used in carbon-fibre reinforced epoxy resin for tennis racquets.
- **Melamine** is used in laminate flooring in indoor sports facilities.
- **Polyester resin** is used in glass-reinforced polyester (GRP) for skis, surfboards and boats.

Properties of Polymers

Polymers…

- have **low density** – they are therefore light
- are **flexible** – in some polymers the chains can slide past each other
- have **poor thermal (heat) conductivity** – they are good insulators because there are no free electrons
- have **poor electrical conductivity** – because there are no free electrons.

Sports Science

Metals

Metals can be either **pure metals**, for example, tin, zinc and iron, or **alloys**, for example, steel.

Structure

Metals have a giant structure in which electrons in the outer energy shells are free to move through the whole structure. This results in a regular arrangement (lattice) of metal ions surrounded by a 'sea' of electrons.

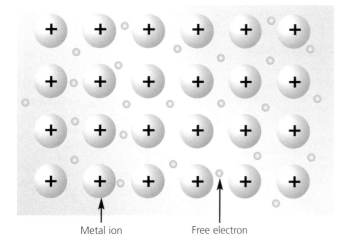

Metal ion   Free electron

Examples and Uses

Steel is used for bicycle components and frames because it has a high tensile strength which enables it to support the cyclist. However, it is quite heavy.

Titanium or aluminium can be used for a bicycle's frame as these metals are less dense (lighter) than steel, however, they are more expensive.

Properties

Metals...

- have **good electrical conductivity** because electrons in the 'sea' are free to move so when a voltage is applied, a current is produced
- have **good thermal (heat) conductivity** because the moving electrons can transfer thermal energy through the metal quickly
- are **hard** – it takes a large force to dent or scratch the surface because there are strong forces between the positive metal ions and the surrounding electrons
- have a **high density** and are therefore heavy because the strong forces between the ions hold them close together
- have a **high tensile strength** (are very strong) – it takes a large force to stretch and break them because there are strong forces between the positive metal ions and the surrounding electrons
- are **malleable (not brittle)** – they can be easily hammered, pressed, rolled or bent into shape, or drawn into a wire because the layers can slide over each other.

Metals in the Periodic Table

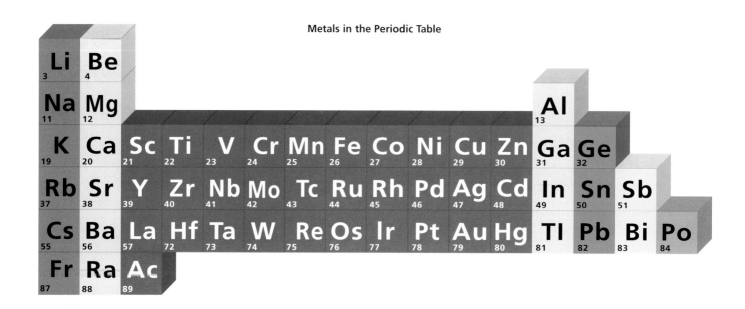

Ceramics

Ceramics are made by heating inorganic compounds (i.e. compounds that do not contain carbon) such as silica, alumina and clay.

Structure

Ceramics are **giant structures** of metallic and non-metallic elements that are held together by either ionic or covalent bonds, depending on the atoms present. In a giant structure (lattice), every atom is bonded to several others around it.

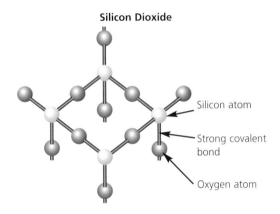

Silicon Dioxide

Silicon atom
Strong covalent bond
Oxygen atom

Examples and Uses

Glass, pottery, china, bricks and cement are all ceramics. They have many uses in the buildings that athletes train in, and as components of composite materials.

Properties

Ceramics…
- are **hard** and **strong** because the lattice is held together by many bonds
- are **brittle** because the atoms cannot slide past each other, which means an applied force breaks the lattice apart
- have a **high melting point** because a lot of energy is needed to break the strong bonds that hold the lattice together
- have **poor thermal conductivity** because the electrons are fixed in bonds and are not free to move
- have **poor electrical conductivity** because the electrons are fixed in bonds and are not free to move.

Composites

Composites are made from two or more different materials, combined together to give the best properties of each.

Structure

Composites can be formed in many ways, for example, they may be in layers, one on top of the other, or one material might be embedded in the 'matrix' of another.

Examples and Uses

GRP (glass-fibre reinforced polyester), or **fibreglass**, is used to make surfboards, boats and skis. It is made of polyester resin, which is much lighter than steel but, because it is brittle, glass fibres are embedded in the resin to strengthen it. Fibreglass is stiff and lightweight.

Carbon-fibre reinforced epoxy resin is used for mountain bikes and tennis racquets. Carbon fibres are embedded in epoxy resin to strengthen it, whilst keeping it lightweight.

Plasticised PVC is used for the soles of trainers. The stiff interlocking PVC molecules have plasticiser molecules between them, so the material becomes flexible.

Properties

Composites are made from a combination of two or more materials, so their properties depend on the properties of the materials they were made from.

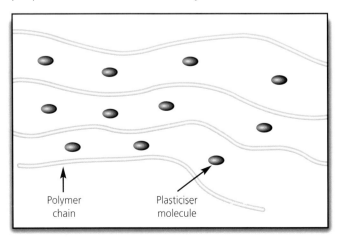

Polymer chain
Plasticiser molecule

Sports Science

Forces

Forces can be pushes, pulls or twists, for example, friction, weight and air resistance. Force is measured in **newtons (N)**.

Whenever two objects are in contact, they exert equal and opposite forces on each other. **Weight** is a downward force caused by the pull of gravity, so there is an upward **reaction force** that is equal and opposite to the downward force (of weight).

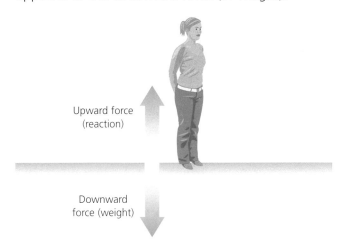

Upward force
(reaction)

Downward
force (weight)

Forces and Movement

Friction is the **force** that resists movement. The force that lets the sole of your shoe grip the ground is **friction**. If there was no friction you would not be able to run, change direction or stop because you could not push off the ground with your foot to start a movement – your foot would just slide across the ground.

The movement or **speed** of an object depends on the forces that are acting on it. For example, the forward **driving force** provided by a cyclist pedalling is opposed by friction between the tyres and the ground, and **air resistance** (see diagram below).

Reducing / Increasing Forces

Athletes choose sports equipment and clothing that have been designed to reduce air resistance and weight to help them move faster.

For example, to reduce **air resistance**, cyclists…
* wear helmets that are smooth and have a **streamlined** shape
* wear tight-fitting clothing to reduce **surface area**
* ride in a crouching position to reduce their surface area.

To reduce weight, cyclists choose clothing and equipment (e.g. bicycles and helmets) that are made from low density (lightweight) materials.

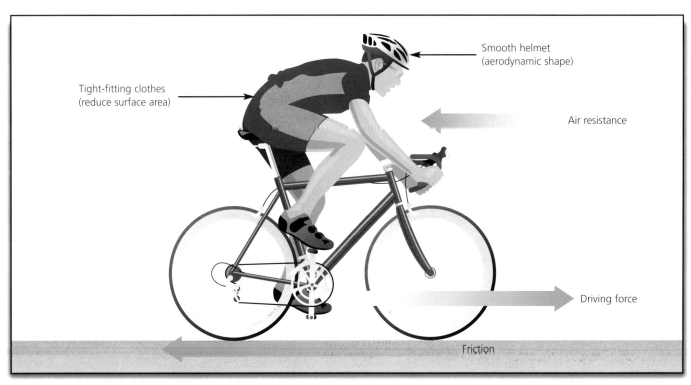

Tight-fitting clothes
(reduce surface area)

Smooth helmet
(aerodynamic shape)

Air resistance

Driving force

Friction

Footwear

Sports footwear is designed to be suitable for different sports which may be played on different surfaces.

The table below summarises the key features of some surfaces:

Surface	Feature
Grass – natural	• Good friction except when wet
Tartan track (for athletics) – synthetic	• All-weather surface • Provides good surface grip, which is improved by wearing footwear with spikes
Astroturf – synthetic	• All-weather surface • Provides good grip (which is why it produces 'burns' on skin)
Wood (for indoor sports) – natural	• Good friction except when wet
Ice – natural	• Poor friction

The grip of a shoe on a surface depends on the **area of contact** the shoe has with the surface. The smaller the area of contact, the greater the force or pressure that is exerted on the surface and the better the grip.

So, the grip of a shoe on different surfaces can be improved by using…
- studs, such as those used in football, rugby and hockey
- spikes, such as those used in athletics, cricket and golf.

Calculating Pressure

The pressure that is exerted on a surface, e.g. the sole of a shoe, can be calculated using the following formula…

$$\text{Pressure (N/cm}^2) = \frac{\text{Force (N)}}{\text{Area (cm}^2)}$$

Example

An athlete weighs 600N. He puts on a pair of shoes.

a) Calculate the pressure he exerts on the ground if he is wearing the stud boots shown below:

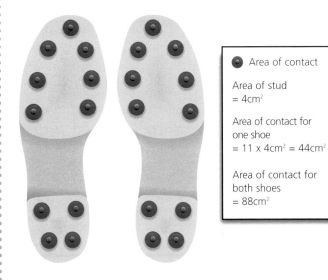

● Area of contact

Area of stud
= 4cm^2

Area of contact for one shoe
= 11 x 4cm^2 = 44cm^2

Area of contact for both shoes
= 88cm^2

Use the formula…

$$\text{Pressure} = \frac{\text{Force}}{\text{Area}}$$

$$= \frac{600\text{N}}{88\text{cm}^2} = \textbf{6.8N/cm}^2$$

b) Calculate the pressure he exerts on the ground if he is wearing the trainers shown below:

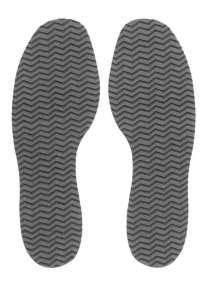

∼ Area of contact

Area of contact for both shoes
= 400cm^2

Use the formula…

$$\text{Pressure} = \frac{\text{Force}}{\text{Area}}$$

$$= \frac{600\text{N}}{400\text{cm}^2} = \textbf{1.5N/cm}^2$$

Sports Science

Sports Clothing

Sports clothing can be made from many materials, depending on the properties that are required.

Materials can be...

- **low density** or **lightweight** – to increase speed
- **durable** – so they do not wear out quickly
- **flexible** – for comfort
- **elastic** – for comfort, and so clothes do not wrinkle when they are stretched
- **waterproof** – so the athlete does not get wet
- **insulating** – to trap air to help maintain the temperature of the body
- **breathable** – so sweat can evaporate and the athlete can lose heat to keep his / her body temperature constant
- **highly absorbent** – to soak up sweat so clothing is more comfortable to wear (see diagram A)
- **not very absorbent** – so clothing does not hold a lot of water or feel sweaty (see diagram B)
- **smooth** – so it is aerodynamic, and to reduce air and water resistance (drag).

A **Wool or cotton**: lots of 'water hooks', lots of water stays attracted to fibre

'Water hook'

Water molecule

Fibre

B **Nylon or polyester**: fewer 'water hooks', less water stays attracted to fibre

---

Gore-Tex® is made from an expanded form of the polymer PTFE. Small amounts of the polymer are used to create a lattice-like structure. It is waterproof because the expanded PTFE is hydrophobic ('water-hating'). It is breathable because a hydrophilic ('water-loving') substance is added to the structure that allows moisture to pass through. It can be laminated to another fabric using either heat or adhesive.

Gore-Tex® is used to make all-weather clothing and shoes, because it is waterproof, windproof and breathable.

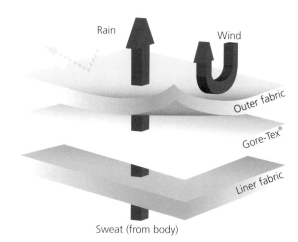

Gore-Tex® Membrane

Rain

Wind

Outer fabric

Gore-Tex®

Liner fabric

Sweat (from body)

Many materials are used to make a trainer:
- Cotton or polyester is used to make the laces because they are flexible and strong.
- Nylon or polyester is used to make the upper part of the shoes, because they are soft and flexible materials.
- Polyurethane foam or gel is used in the sole as a shock absorber because it is spongy.
- Plasticised PVC is used to make the sole because it is flexible and durable.

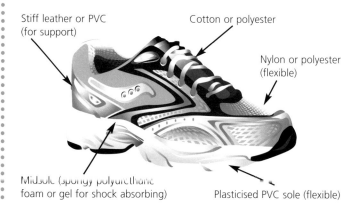

Stiff leather or PVC (for support)

Cotton or polyester

Nylon or polyester (flexible)

Midsole (spongy polyurethane foam or gel for shock absorbing)

Plasticised PVC sole (flexible)

The tables below summarise the advantages, disadvantages and uses of some natural and synthetic materials.

Natural Materials	Advantages	Disadvantages	Used in...
Cotton	• High water absorbency • Strong	• Dries slowly • Creases easily	• Martial arts suits • Shorts • T-shirts • Underwear
Leather	• Strong	• Heavy • Cracks if not treated with wax	• Boots • Boxing gloves • Motorcycle jackets
Silk	• Lightweight • Breathable	• Expensive	• Boxing shorts • Thermal underwear
Wool	• Good insulator • High water absorbency	• Heavy • Dries slowly	• Gloves • Hats • Jumpers • Socks

Synthetic Materials	Advantages	Disadvantages	Used in...
Gore-Tex® (PTFE polymer membrane)	• Waterproof • Breathable • Lightweight	• Expensive	• Hats • Jackets • Shoe linings
Lycra	• Elastic • Durable	• Feels sweaty	• Active wear, e.g. running suits, wetsuits
Microfibre	• Good insulator • Lightweight	• Low strength • High water absorbency	• Gloves • Hats • Jackets • Jumpers
Nylon	• Lightweight • Dries quickly • Low water absorbency	• Damaged by long exposure to sunlight	• Swimwear
Polyester	• Dries quickly • Low water absorbency • Does not stretch • Does not crease	• Feels sweaty	• Active wear, e.g. running suits, swimwear • T-shirts
Polypropylene	• Lightweight	• Feels sweaty	• Thermal underwear
PVC	• Waterproof • Flexible	• Feels sweaty	• Hats • Jackets • Swimwear • Trainers

Sports Science

Sports Equipment

Sports equipment is made from a wide range of materials, which are chosen depending on the properties that are required.

Wood was originally used to make tennis racquets, cricket bats, hockey sticks, skis and surfboards. As a result, they were heavy, absorbed water and sometimes split. However, materials scientists have since developed new materials which have much better properties.

Today, sports equipment is often made from composites which have glass or carbon fibres trapped in a polymer resin. These materials are lightweight (not very dense), stiff and strong and are not damaged if they come into contact with water.

Tennis racquets are now made from new composite materials. For example, the frame could be made from carbon fibres in epoxy resin. This makes it light yet stiff and strong.

Most **bicycle frames** are made of steel but some are made from aluminium alloy which is much less dense, and therefore lighter, than steel. Expensive racing bicycles may be made from carbon fibres trapped in a polymer resin. These are strong yet lightweight.

Footballs and rugby balls used to be made of leather. Today they are made of polyester cotton and synthetic rubber which are laminated together. This makes them lighter, more streamlined, and more durable.

Protective Equipment

Materials have also been developed to be used for protective equipment, such as cycling, riding and ski helmets, and shin pads. These new materials benefit the athlete by being very strong and yet lightweight. They may also have improved safety features, such as cushioned linings to reduce the effects of impact on the body.

Tennis Racquets

Bicycle Frame

Footballs and Rugby Balls

Protective Equipment

Example Question

For Unit 2 you will sit a one-hour exam with structured questions. An annotated example question is shown below.

1   Blood samples can be found at some crime scenes.

(a) Describe a method that can be used to lift a sample of blood from a crime scene.

Use a cotton bud to lift a sample of the blood. Then place it inside a sterile container.

(1 mark)

(b) A sample of blood was analysed to determine the blood group.

The results of the test are shown in the table below:

Test	Result
Mixed with Anti-A antibodies	Blood cells clumped together
Mixed with Anti-B antibodies	Blood cells did not clump

Which blood group was the blood sample?

Blood group A

(1 mark)

(c) Blood can be analysed to find out information about a person.

(i) Give one example, apart from blood group, of the type of information that can be found by analysing a blood sample.

A DNA profile

(1 mark)

(ii) Describe the technique used to find out this information.

Extracts of DNA are taken from the blood sample.

The DNA is then cut into fragments using enzymes.

The DNA is then separated by gel electrophoresis.

The negatively charged DNA fragments move towards the positive electrode.

A radioactive substance is then used to label the DNA fragments.

The fragments are then X-rayed.

(4 marks)

1 This requires you to recall the procedure used for taking blood samples.
2 This question requires you to interpret the information given in the table.
3 This requires you to recall further information about blood analysis.
4 Make sure you describe the stages of the processes in detail.
5 There are six points you can make; all are included in the answer shown. However, you only need to make four points in order to get four marks.

Glossary

Accuracy – refers to the properties of a measuring instrument. For example, a voltmeter may have an accuracy of 10%, which means that a reading of 3.0V represents a voltage of 3.0V ± 0.3V (2.7–3.3V)

Acid – a substance that dissolves in water to form a solution with a pH below 7; a substance that contains $H^+_{(aq)}$ ions when dissolved in water; a substance that neutralises an alkali

Alkali – a substance that dissolves in water to form a solution with a pH above 7; a substance that contains $OH^-_{(aq)}$ ions when dissolved in water; a substance that neutralises an acid

Alloy – a metal made by heating together two or more metals, for example, steel (an alloy of iron and carbon)

Antibodies – proteins that neutralise the effect of antigens; produced by white blood cells

Atom – the smallest particle of an element which can exist

Boiling point – the temperature at which a liquid turns to a gas

Catalyst – a substance that makes a reaction speed up without being changed

Cell – the basic unit of living organisms; consists of a nucleus, cytoplasm and a membrane

Chromosome – composed of DNA and protein; each chromosome consists of a series of genes

Compound – a substance in which the atoms of two or more elements are chemically joined, either by ionic or covalent bonds

Concentration – of an aqueous solution is the number of moles of solute in $1dm^3$ of solution (mol dm^{-3} or M). $1dm^3$ = 1 litre or $1000cm^3$

Conduction – i) electrical conduction – takes place when charged particles move through a material; ii) thermal conduction – takes place when energy is transferred from energetic particles to less energetic neighbouring particles by vibrations and collisions

Conductor – a material that allows charged particles or thermal energy to flow through it

Crystal – a piece of solid substance that has a regular shape, flat sides, sharp edges and angles

Current – the flow of electric charge. The current in a metallic conductor is due to a flow of negatively charged electrons

DCPIP (dichlorophenolindophenol) – a blue chemical that can be used as a dye

Density (of a material) – the mass per unit volume; measured in units of g/cm^3 or kg/m^3

Diffusion – the movement of a substance from an area where it is in high concentration to an area of lower concentration along a concentration gradient; bigger the difference in concentration, the steeper the concentration gradient and the faster the rate of diffusion

Dissolving – the process that takes place when a solute is added to a solvent and the solute disappears; the particles of solute fit between the particles of solvent

Efficiency – a measure of the proportion or percentage of energy input that is transferred to a useful energy output; it is a ratio; it does not have a unit

Elastic – the property of a material that can return to its original size and shape when the force causing it to deform is removed

Electrons – the outermost particles in atoms; they orbit the nucleus and have a negative charge

Element – a pure substance made of one kind of atom

Enzymes – biological catalysts (proteins) which speed up the rate of reaction in living cells

Eutrophication – excessive growth of algae due to enrichment of water with minerals from fertilisers, which results in death of water plants due to lack of light. Microorganisms decompose the plants and, as they respire, they remove oxygen from the water causing fish and other animals to die due to lack of oxygen

Glossary

Evaporation – the process by which a liquid changes to a gas due to particles leaving the surface of the liquid. This happens at temperatures below the boiling point, but is fastest when the liquid is boiling

Excretion – the process of getting rid of waste products, such as urea and carbon dioxide, from the body

Fermentation – a process which produces alcohol and carbon dioxide

Filtering – a method of separating a solid from a liquid

Gas – a state of matter where the particles have a lot of energy and are widely spaced

Gene – a section of DNA which, on its own or with other genes, codes for a characteristic of an organism

Homogenous – same consistency throughout

Hormone – a chemical compound, e.g. insulin, glucagon, secreted directly into the bloodstream by ductless glands, which affects target organs elsewhere in the body

Ion – a molecule or atom which has a positive (cation) or negative (anion) electrical charge

Liquid – a state of matter where the particles are close together, irregularly arranged and able to move over each other

Mass – the amount of material that makes up the object; measured in kilograms (kg)

Melting point – the temperature at which a solid changes to a liquid

Monomer – a small molecule which forms the building block to make a polymer

Neutralisation – a reaction in which an acid reacts with an alkali to form a neutral product

Oxidation – a reaction which involves at least one of the following: the loss of electrons, the gain of oxygen or the loss of hydrogen

pH – a measure of the acidity or alkalinity of a substance

Polymer – a long-chain molecule built up from small units called monomers

Quantitative test – used to find the amount of a substance present in a sample

Qualitative test – used to find out whether a substance is present in a sample

Redox reaction – a reaction where both reduction and oxidation are taking place

Reduction – a reaction which involves at least one of the following: gain of electrons, the loss of oxygen or the gain of hydrogen

Reliability – the consistency of a measurement, or measuring instruments

Respiration – the process which takes place in the living cells of all plants and animals which releases energy

Solid – a state of matter where there are strong forces of attraction between the particles; it cannot be compressed

Solution – the mixture formed when a solute dissolves in a solvent

Speed – how fast an object travels; measured in metres per second (m/s)

Standard solution – a solution which has a known concentration

Temperature – a measure of how hot an object is; measured in degrees Celcius (°C)

Titration – an accurate technique which can be used to find the volume of liquid needed to neutralise an acid or decolourise DCPIP

Weight – the gravitational force that pulls an object towards the centre of the planet. On the surface of Earth, each kilogram of mass has a weight of approximately 10N

Index

Acknowledgements

The author and publisher would like to thank everyone who has contributed to this book:

IFC   ©iStockphoto.com / Andrei Tchernov
p.11   ©iStockphoto.com / Yale Bernstein
p.37   ©iStockphoto.com / Yale Bernstein
p.46   ©iStockphoto.com / Peter Galbraith
p.64   ©iStockphoto.com / Yale Bernstein
p.74   ©iStockphoto.com

ISBN-10: 1-905129-67-X
ISBN-13: 978-1-905129-67-6

Published by Lonsdale, a division of Huveaux Plc

Project Editor: Rachael Hemsley
Cover and Concept Design: Sarah Duxbury
Designer: Richard Arundale
Artwork: Lonsdale and HL Studios

Periodic Table

Key

Mass number →

Atomic number (Proton number) →

1		
H		
hydrogen		
1		

Group 1	Group 2	Group 3	Group 4	Group 5	Group 6	Group 7	Group 8 or 0
							4 **He** helium 2
7 **Li** lithium 3	9 **Be** beryllium 4	11 **B** boron 5	12 **C** carbon 6	14 **N** nitrogen 7	16 **O** oxygen 8	19 **F** fluorine 9	20 **Ne** neon 10
23 **Na** sodium 11	24 **Mg** magnesium 12	27 **Al** aluminium 13	28 **Si** silicon 14	31 **P** phosphorus 15	32 **S** sulfur 16	35 **Cl** chlorine 17	40 **Ar** argon 18
39 **K** potassium 19	40 **Ca** calcium 20	45 **Sc** scandium 21	48 **Ti** titanium 22	51 **V** vanadium 23	52 **Cr** chromium 24	55 **Mn** manganese 25	(transition metals)
56 **Fe** iron 26	59 **Co** cobalt 27	59 **Ni** nickel 28	63 **Cu** copper 29	64 **Zn** zinc 30	70 **Ga** gallium 31	73 **Ge** germanium 32	75 **As** arsenic 33
79 **Se** selenium 34	80 **Br** bromine 35	84 **Kr** krypton 36					
85 **Rb** rubidium 37	88 **Sr** strontium 38	89 **Y** yttrium 39	91 **Zr** zirconium 40	93 **Nb** niobium 41	96 **Mo** molybdenum 42	98 **Tc** technetium 43	101 **Ru** ruthenium 44
103 **Rh** rhodium 45	106 **Pd** palladium 46	108 **Ag** silver 47	112 **Cd** cadmium 48	115 **In** indium 49	119 **Sn** tin 50	122 **Sb** antimony 51	128 **Te** tellurium 52
127 **I** iodine 53	131 **Xe** xenon 54						
133 **Cs** caesium 55	137 **Ba** barium 56	139 **La** lanthanum 57	178 **Hf** hafnium 72	181 **Ta** tantalum 73	184 **W** tungsten 74	186 **Re** rhenium 75	190 **Os** osmium 76
192 **Ir** iridium 77	195 **Pt** platinum 78	197 **Au** gold 79	201 **Hg** mercury 80	204 **Tl** thallium 81	207 **Pb** lead 82	209 **Bi** bismuth 83	210 **Po** polonium 84
210 **At** astatine 85	222 **Rn** radon 86						
223 **Fr** francium 87	226 **Ra** radium 88	227 **Ac** actinium 89					

Lanthanides

140 **Ce** cerium 58	141 **Pr** praseodymium 59	144 **Nd** neodymium 60	147 **Pm** promethium 61	150 **Sm** samarium 62	152 **Eu** europium 63	157 **Gd** gadolinium 64	159 **Tb** terbium 65	162 **Dy** dysprosium 66	165 **Ho** holmium 67	167 **Er** erbium 68	169 **Tm** thulium 69	173 **Yb** ytterbium 70	175 **Lu** lutetium 71
232 **Th** thorium 90	231 **Pa** protactinium 91	238 **U** uranium 92	237 **Np** neptunium 93	242 **Pu** plutonium 94	243 **Am** americium 95	247 **Cm** curium 96	247 **Bk** berkelium 97	251 **Cf** californium 98	254 **Es** einsteinium 99	253 **Fm** fermium 100	256 **Md** mendelevium 101	254 **No** nobelium 102	257 **Lw** lawrencium 103

The lines of elements going across are called periods.

The columns of elements going down are called groups.